CEDAR CREST COLLEGE LIBRARY
ALLENTOWN. PA. 18104

teaching
the
young
child

teaching the young child

susan rounds

a handbook of classroom practice

agathon press, new york

© 1975, 1987 by Susan Rounds

Published by
Agathon Press, Inc.
111 Eighth Avenue
New York, NY 10011

Illustrations by The Whole Works

All rights reserved

No portion of this book may be reproduced by any process, stored in a retrieval system, or transmitted in any form, or by any means, without the express written permission of the publisher.

Library of Congress Cataloging-in-Publication Data

Rounds, Susan.
    Teaching the young child.

    Bibliography; p.
    Includes index.
    1. Activity programs in education—United States—
Handbooks, manuals, etc.   2. Education, Elementary—
United States—Handbooks, manuals, etc.   3. Teaching—
Handbooks, manuals, etc.   I. Title.
LB1027.25.R68   1987   372.13   86-28861
ISBN 0-87586-079-6
ISBN 0-87586-073-7 (pbk.)

This is a substantially revised version of the original edition, first published in 1975.

Printed in the United States of America

contents

1

what this book is about

Recently one mother confided to me that her five-year-old daughter had started off to school in September full of eagerness and enthusiasm, thrilled to finally be able to to to school. But after only two weeks of lock-step everyone-turn-to-page-three instruction, and of countless take-home dittoes that were variations on the same theme, and that were much too easy for her, she began asking her mother wearily, "Do I really have to go to school?"

In spite of all that is known about the conditions under which young children learn best, it is unfortunately still all too common to find kindergarten classrooms with twenty-five or thirty youngsters sitting at tables going through workbooks page by page under the teacher's step-by-step instruction. In classrooms such as these, children quickly become bored and disillusioned about school and learning.

This book has been written to show that there is an alternative for children and teachers. It is a book for teachers who have become dissatisfied with the "quality of life" in their classrooms, and who want to create a classroom environment that sparks their own interest and enthusiasm as much as it does the children's. It is a practical, down-to-earth guide written by one who has been there herself, and has found practical help sadly lacking. It describes how to set up what I call an activity-centered classroom. As the name implies, this classroom is centered upon children's activity; but that activity is not random. Rather, the environment has been carefully structured by the teacher so that learning becomes virtually inevitable, because it capitalizes on children's enthusiasm and interest. I have tried to offer concrete ideas for the organization of an activity-centered classroom, to suggest possible units of study, to describe many independent activities that the children can undertake, and to outline ways of keeping records of what the children are doing. There are chapters that explain how reading and mathematics are presented in an activity-centered classroom. Art and cooking projects are also described.

I have drawn the practical examples for instruction from my own experience in running an activity-centered kindergarten classroom in New York State, but the teaching methods and many of the specific activities apply equally well to the first and second grade. While kindergarten teachers can use this book as the basis for their program, first and second grade teachers will find it most useful as a supplemental handbook that will provide new ideas for classroom organization and instructional techniques. Further, reading readiness instruction is as important to first grade teachers as it is to kindergarten teachers, and in fact, a number of the reading readiness skills discussed in Chapter Two will not be appropriate for many children until they reach first grade. The math learning activities presented in Chapter Three can be presented to first grade children as a supplement to their prescribed assignments in a math textbook. The remaining chapters are appropriate to any primary classroom.

What is the pattern of a school day in an activity-centered kindergarten classroom? There is a brief opening time, where the Pledge of Allegiance may be said, and business details such as attendance and collection of money for trips are taken care of, and then a discussion of the day's activity is held. There follows a long activity period, of from one to one and a half hours, when the children are free to choose from among a wide variety of activities. They may sort and count acorns, buttons or seeds; make simple graphs reflecting the number of girls and boys present and absent; listen to records; or measure salt and flour for making play dough. They may retell a favorite story using a flannel board, paint pictures at the easel, dictate stories about their paintings to an adult, or make a book about the number 3. They may use a magnifying glass to examine a collection of feathers, or compare the height of two bean plants grown under different conditions. As they move from one activity to another, children may work by themselves, with another child, or in small groups, either with or without the teacher or another adult. It is the time when most of the "work" of the class is done. The day concludes with a period of outdoor play or other organized physical activity, followed by a closing time with music, stories, and perhaps some quiet games.

In such a classroom, play and work become virtually indistinguishable, as children choose from a rich and varied offering of learning experiences that have been carefully planned and structured by the teacher. They are talking, thinking, experiencing, sharing, creating, learning. The classroom is not silent, but it is never noisy. Rather, it is characterized by the pleasant hum of children's voices as they talk quietly to themselves, to other children engaged in the same activity, or to the teacher. The classroom is a busy, interesting, comfortable place to be. Visitors to the classroom are impressed with the children's involvement in their work, and by their ability to finish a task, then move on to another one without adult direction.

An important feature of this approach is that the teacher sees each child as an individual with his or her own learning style and unique needs. There is a careful balance between activities that develop academic skills, and activities such as block play, dramatic play, and painting, which have always been considered essential to good early childhood education. As a result, the classroom can comfortably accommodate and provide challenges appropriate to children at many different levels of development. Freed from the frustrations of trying to teach the same material to large groups of children all at once, the teacher is able to keep track of the progress of each child in many different areas, and so is ready to help an individual child with the appropriate instruction at the appropriate time. The teacher also recognizes that children are the most powerful enhancers of their own learning, and that the intensity of their involvement—their engagement with the task at hand—is an important determinant of the quality of their educational experience.

If your present classroom is quite traditional, and you are unsure about how to begin to change, you can begin gradually by allowing the children one free period during the day when they can choose from among painting, math activities, creative writing, and other activities. As you and the children learn to use the activity-centered time, you can gradually extend it. That was how I started in my own kindergarten room. As long as you give yourself and the children time to learn and explore and the freedom to make choices about things that matter, you will end up with a successful program.

What are the results of individually structured activity-centered learning in the classroom? Academically, it appears to be a much more effective way of learning. Children do not waste time going over material that is too hard or too easy for them. It provides you as a teacher with many opportunities to get to know your children as individuals. You are able to tailor your teaching approach to the learning style of each child, using a kinesthetic approach with one child, a slow pace with much repetition with another, and challenging material and a faster pace with yet another. You can use small group instruction effectively because you know which children are ready for a particular skill at the same time. You can encourage children to help each other learn so that they do not need to rely exclusively on the teacher.

The classroom environment furnishes ideal conditions for children to grow in all aspects of language. It is an environment which provides a sharp contrast to the familiar pattern of teacher-child interaction in so many classrooms, in which the conversational ball bounces from teacher to child A, back to the teacher, then to child B, back to the teacher, then to child C, and so forth. The teacher's questions are, of course, well-formed sentences, but children's responses are predominantly one or two-word phrases and incomplete sentences. In situations like these, children are hard put to increase their control over language, or to learn to use it in more complex ways. In the activity-centered classroom, on the other hand, children test out their ideas by talking to one another, and by describing what they are doing to interested adults. They learn that what they say is important, because the teacher listens to them, encourages them to talk, and often writes down what they say. They see the value of written language demonstrated for them every day in many ways—when the teacher writes down a recipe they will follow in making a classroom snack; when she labels their block structures for them, or helps them to make their own labels; when they dictate stories to an adult and begin to learn how the words they say are related to those mysterious marks on paper. All these activities help them to make those important connections between doing, talking about, and listening on the one hand, and reading and writing on the other hand. These connections are the foundations of literacy. They are crucial for later success in school.

There are also many social and emotional gains to be made from the experiences of an activity-centered classroom. First, there is much less competition among children, because they are working on many different things at the same time and thus do not have the opportunity to watch other children struggle over material that they can do with ease. In addition, competition among parents is reduced. The fierce struggle evident in school systems where I have taught can be very destructive to children as well as to parents. But when you do not feed that hunger by refusing to give out the standardized work that allows Susie's parents to beam with pleasure when she has circled every triangle on her page while Mary has missed three, you can redirect parents' interest by showing them how their child is progressing and learning at his or her own speed and constantly mastering important skills.

Because there is a lot of cooperative interaction in the room, relationships between children are encouraged, and dependence on the teacher is discouraged. You will also find that discipline becomes much less of a problem. There are fewer points of conflict between recalcitrant children and the teacher in her role as organizer and director of the class, because the children have many opportunities to be involved in vigorous activity instead of being forced to remain quiet for long periods of time.

Because children in this kind of classroom are able to choose from many different activities, they learn to make decisions, to manage their time, to be responsible for their own behavior. They become more independent, more self-reliant, more ready to take the initiative. Most parents are thrilled with the maturity that they see developing throughout the year. As children are given more and more responsibility, they become more and more capable of handling it. As they are given a variety of stimulating and interesting things to do, they become more active participants in their own educational process, instead of being passive consumers of instruction given *ex cathedra* by the teacher.

Perhaps more important than any other single achievement, the activity-centered classroom gives the kindergarten child that enthusiasm for learning and for going to school which is a prerequisite for success in later education. In fact, it lays a large burden on the teachers who follow you in your pupils' careers. If they have learned from you that school is an exciting place to learn about themselves and the world around them, a place they were eager to return to every Monday morning, and were sorry to leave at the end of the year, woe betide teachers who force them into disillusionment!

How to Set Up Your Classroom and Begin

If you are reading this book well before the opening of a new school year, there are a number of things you can do to prepare yourself for a more activity-oriented arrangement in the fall. If schools are still in session, try to arrange with your principal to visit schools in your area that already have established programs such as the one you are considering. More can be learned in a few hours at a school that is actually doing the things you

are interested in than in days of study. As you visit, take
note of room arrangements, of ideas for projects, and
of other things you might be able to use. If you have not
already ordered your materials for the coming year, you
may want to consider adding or subtracting things on
the basis of your new plans. Do you have enough art
materials, do you have too many workbooks? Also,
compile a list of materials for use in your room that
parents can save for you over the summer. Send the list
home with the children in June. Some materials you
might include are listed in Appendix C.

During the summer, think about units you would like
to work with. Perhaps you have units you have taught
as whole-group lessons that can be adapted to a more
individual approach. Two units, one on American Indian life, and the other on health and the body, are
included in this book. Some other topics of interest to
small children are the seashore, animals, circuses,
machines and tools, outer space, and transportation.
You should collect pictures and ideas for projects so
you will have some of the preparation done before you
begin teaching.

Prepare some independent games and activities to increase the supply you may already have in your room.
Suggestions for them are given in later chapters.

Think about how you will rearrange your room. The
layout is extremely important, and you will probably
not hit on the right arrangement until after several
trials. You will want to have interest centers where the
children can go to pursue particular kinds of activities.
Some of these will remain the same throughout the
year and others will be temporary, but the more varied
and interesting these centers are, the more successful
your program will be.

In order to have as many different centers as possible,
it is sometimes necessary to go outside your classroom
in search of available space. If you have a hall outside
your room, it can be put to good use as a setting for
your easels. Wooden building-blocks can be brought
out into the hall and stored in their cabinet there. An
old rug can be laid down next to the cabinet to cut
down on the noise of the blocks on the bare floor. The

playhouse can be set up in a corner of the hall. Here will be placed the child-sized furniture, such as stove, refrigerator, table and chairs, and the dolls. Remember the boys when you equip your playhouse. Include some men's hats and ties in the costume box, and a safety razor without a blade and a mirror for shaving practice. A workbench with child-sized tools and scrap lumber can be placed in the hall to be used whenever you have an older person to supervise it. At various times during the year the hall can also serve as the location of a grocery store, a puppet theatre, and a place to do large-scale art projects such as murals and mosaics. If it is absolutely impossible for you to use space outside your room, you can rotate interest centers inside your room during the year so that all are included at one time or another.

One interest center which you may find convenient is a snack table. Instead of an everybody-eats-at-once snack period, try a serve-yourself arrangement. A table and three chairs are set aside for the snack, and supplied each morning with several cans of fruit juice, a box of crackers, a can opener, a pitcher, and paper cups. When the snack table is always available to the children, they are able to eat when they are hungry and they take care of the maintenance themselves, putting out more juice and crackers when they are needed. At first you will have to open the cans of juice and pour them into the pitchers whenever the pitcher is empty. As the year progresses the children will be able to assume this responsibility as well. You will want to lay down some ground rules at the beginning of the year when the table is introduced, specifying how many children are to be at the table at once, how much juice and how many crackers they may have, and how often they may visit the table during the session. If you have a large class, you will want to limit each child to one trip to the table; otherwise there will not be time for everyone to have a snack during the morning. Make the children responsible for keeping the table neat and clean.

The library corner will be an important part of your room all year, so allocate a generous space for it. A small rug, pieces of carpeting, pillows, an overstuffed chair, and a big stuffed animal will all make the corner even more appealing. Low shelves and tables should be plentifully supplied with a variety of picture books, familiar stories, and magazines. A record player can be equipped with four earphones so that children may listen to recordings of songs and stories without disturbing the rest of the class. Several publishers, including Scholastic Books, Weston Woods, and Scott, Foresman, provide sets of records and books that go together so that the child can follow the story in the book as he listens to it read on the record. Weston Woods, in particular, has filmstrips of the stories as well, so that you can show the filmstrips to the class one day, and then place the book and record in the library corner for them to listen to again on their own. Slide viewers and slides for the children to look at can be placed in the library area. An old typewriter can be placed on a table with sheets of newsprint for children to use. They will be fascinated with pounding the keys to make letters appear, and some of them will move on to type out the alphabet, their names, and other words they can spell.

The art corner, like the library corner, can remain basically the same throughout the year, except that some of the contents may be varied. This section should have tables and chairs for perhaps ten children to sit and work. On shelves convenient to the children's reach are stored drawing paper of various sizes and types, including sheets of newspaper (want ads in particular make good backgrounds for painting, chalk, and charcoal work), crayons, paste, pencils, paper and material scraps, scissors, and oaktag outlines of shapes for the child to trace. As often as you can, every other day or so, set out a specific project for children to work on in addition to whatever free use of the materials they may make. Sometimes the project might be the use of a particular material, such as play dough or chalk or watercolors. Sometimes it might be connected to the unit you are working on (Indian vests, clown collages, Santa Claus mobile, pictures of outer space, and so forth).

Another corner of the room can house the cooking area. The basic requirement here is a place to store your cooking equipment so that it is safely out of the children's way except when a cooking project is under way. When you are ready to cook, the equipment can be moved to a convenient table for the duration of the project.

The science center will contain the animals you wish to keep in your room—gerbils, hamsters, goldfish, rabbits, turtles. Children can contribute interesting items to share, such as rocks, beautiful leaves, cocoons, skeletons of animals found in the woods, and birds' nests. Several magnifying glasses can be left here for children to use in examining the displays. Other material may be added to the center during the study of various units (a map of the solar system during a unit on space travel, plastic models of teeth, ears, and other parts of the body during a unit on health, various seeds and pictures of the plants they came from, during a unit on growing things).

The math area should, like the art corner, contain space for tables and chairs so that several children may sit down to work with the variety of materials to be found here. These will include an assortment of puzzles ranging in difficulty from simple to fairly complex. Many kindergarten children enjoy working on hundred-piece puzzles such as you can purchase inexpensively in the dime store. Perhaps you can trade off puzzles with another teacher in order to increase your supply. Pegboards and pegs of various colors, along with pattern cards showing designs to be made, can be placed on another shelf, as well as wooden beads in various colors and sizes with shoelaces to string them on. Magnetic numerals, wooden numerals, and number charts should be available. Boxes of objects for counting, follow-the-dot papers, scales and balances, and various measuring devices are other materials that should be put out in this area from time to time.

The following description of a typical kindergarten day is based on my former classroom in Chappaqua, New York. It describes how things went after the children were well acquainted with each other and the program.

The day began as the children arrived from the buses and took off their coats. Because their arrival was staggered over twenty minutes, and I liked to keep the children together as a group to begin the day, this time was often used for singing. The children learned many songs that they liked to sing to guitar or piano accompaniment, so these first few minutes passed quickly. On days when we did not sing, we played games or read stories until everyone had arrived.

When all the children had arrived, we said the pledge of allegiance, took the attendance, discussed the date and the weather, and then set about the business of the day. At the end of the opening discussion, I would describe some of the options that would be available to them during the free activity period, which usually lasted about ninety minutes. Some involved working with an adult, others were available for them to do with other children or by themselves. Some of the options were always available and quite familiar to the children so they did not need to be reviewed every day. At this point I would always encourage them to choose a particular activity to start out with and to tell me what they had chosen. Then, as the free period began, each child would leave the group to begin what he or she had chosen, and from that point on, move from one activity to another by choice.

By themselves or with friends the children could listen to the record player, look at library books, type on the old typewriter, look at slides, play in the playhouse, build in the block corner, play the piano, have a snack, play at the water or the sand table, work in the art center with clay or on some other project, do puzzles, work with pegboards, observe the animals, or help make cookies. Not all of these activities were available every day. Variety is essential in order to maintain interest. Thus, the puzzles were rotated, the water table was put away for awhile and then brought out again, different art materials were available at different times, and so forth.

Activities in which adults helped included the children's dictating their own creative stories, working on reading skills, carrying out science and math activities that needed some direction, working on special art, woodworking or cooking projects that required adult help, and various educational games.

Since we had activities going on in the hall as well as in the room, we devised a checkout system that let us control the number of children who were out of the room at any one time and also enabled the children to see whether there was room for them at a particular hall activity without consulting me. It worked this way:

The hall activities were snack, which could take three at a time; the playhouse, which could take four; the big blocks, which could take four; and two easels, which could take two each. We hung a pegboard inside the classroom door with four labels, each printed in a different color: SNACK, BLOCKS, HOUSE, PAINTS. Underneath each label was a peg on which hung three or four round tags colored to match the word they belonged to. Underneath each peg were the correct number of empty pegs, three for snack, four for all the rest. If a child wanted to go out to snack, he went to the board, took down a yellow tag, and placed it on one of the empty pegs. When he finished his snack, he was responsible for returning his tag to its resting place. In this way the children could check the board and see which activities were vacant without asking the teacher. It did require training—helping them to remember which tags represented which activities and reminding them to be careful about placing and returning their tags conscientiously. Every now and then we would find a child out in the hall who had simply wandered out, or who had forgotten to come back in after he had finished with the activity he had signed up for. He had to return to the room, and we explained to the children why it was necessary to limit the number who could be in the hall at once.

In any class, there will be a few who cannot do well apart from direct adult supervision. I once had a child who disappeared whenever he was allowed to work in the hall. Firmer limits must be placed on such children than are placed on the others. They cannot be expected to make responsible choices, and so the options available to them should be limited. As they become more able to cope with freedom, their options can be expanded. Despite some difficulties, hall programs can work very smoothly. Children enjoy assuming responsibility for maintaining the system themselves, which allows them to be more independent of the teacher. Using the hall for some of your activities will free more space in the classroom, and it will also make the room quieter, since anywhere from three to twelve children may be out of the room at once. The hall is a place where children can be a little noisier, and where they can move around without adults hovering around. Many children need that, even if it is for just a few minutes; soon, they will wander back in, ready to begin something in the room.

At the end of the long activity period in our classroom, we would go outside, weather permitting, or have organized games in the room. Music and a story concluded the day.

The first few days of school will involve not nearly so complex a program as the one just described. The children will have to learn the routine and get used to you and to being at school. Experienced teachers have their own ways of introducing children to kindergarten. The only difference in introducing them to an informal classroom will be your showing them how to use the interest centers and getting them used to working by themselves for longer and longer periods of time.

During the first few days, after your opening time, you will want to have a variety of activities that are familiar to the children, such as crayons, puzzles, and blocks. Encourage them to move from one activity to another. You will need to spend this time walking around, helping them, talking to them, seeing that they are finding things to do. During the first days, it is best to keep the activity period shorter than you will eventually want to have it. Kindergarten children are timid and unsure of themselves at first and need more guidance and organization than they will need later on. Therefore you should have plenty of other activities planned in addition to the free time in the room—a walk around the school, time on the playground, a songfest, a movie, familiar games, stories, and so forth. You may want to have snack in a group during the first few days and only gradually introduce the independent snack table.

Once the children have become accustomed to the idea of working by themselves and as they settle into the routine, you can begin to work with individuals, perhaps on a skills inventory as suggested in the chapter on reading readiness. When you approach a child for the purpose of working with you on something such as the inventory, he may already be involved in an activity. You may be able to find another child to work with and come back to the first child a little later when he is finished, but there will be times when you will have to interrupt him. Rather than ask, Would you like to come over and do this with me? which may force him into making a negative decision, since he doesn't know exactly what will be involved, simply tell him, It's time for you to come over and do something with me now. This will work very well *if* the child knows that he will be free to return to the activity he was pursuing after he has finished with you; *if* the activities you ask him to do are appropriate and interesting; *if* you are flexible enough to make exceptions when the situation warrants.

Getting Help

As you work gradually into your program, you may become frustrated by wanting to do more things with the children than you can do by yourself. Cooking projects, art projects, working on stories, making graphs—there are many activities going on at once and not enough time to get everything done. In the most wealthy and enlightened districts, and in some poor districts aided by Federal funds, teacher aides are not uncommon. I was blessed one year with an extremely competent full-time aide, and it certainly made a difference. Barring a sudden change of heart among dispensers of public money, most kindergarten teachers will probably have to do without an aide for many more years. But there is a way you can take some of the pressure off yourself and enhance the program you can offer your children; that is, to get volunteers into your room.

Who is available to help out in your classroom? Investigate the possibility of asking senior citizens to read stories or help with art and woodworking projects. High school students may be able to join the classroom during the day as part of a home economics program. High school shop students may be able to supervise the woodworking table. And parents can be your single best source of volunteer help.

Many teachers I have talked to express strong misgivings about inviting parents to come into the room on an informal basis. They feel that they will always be on the spot, and will worry if the day does not go very smoothly. These are natural feelings, for as teachers we are constantly in the public eye as custodians of parents' most precious possessions. I had many similar feelings when I first asked the class mothers in my room to ask parents to volunteer as aides. But I was desperate. I was very anxious to do more than I could do by myself and there was simply no money available to pay for help. And once I had gotten over my initial fears, everything went very much better than I had expected. Of course, there were one or two parents who questioned what I was doing, but the great majority of mothers became enthusiastic partisans, once they had a chance to see for themselves exactly what was going on. And let's face it: no matter what kind of program you run, and no matter how hard you work, you will always find a tiny minority of parents who will criticize you no matter what you do. I think you will find that working more closely with the parents will allow you to get to know them better and will facilitate much better parent-teacher relationships. In addition, as more people participate in your classroom program, knowledge of what the school is doing will increase, lines of communication will be opened, and relations between the school and the community will be improved. In one school district where I taught, parents were so pleased with the results of activity-centered classrooms that they petitioned the school board to expand the program to other grades and schools.

What sorts of things can you ask parents to help with? I felt that I did not want parents working on academic skills with their own or other children because there were too many possibilities for tension there. But art projects, embroidery, cooking, woodworking, going on class trips, taking down creative stories, and reading stories aloud were all things that mothers enjoyed doing. And the children loved having their mothers in school every so often. Only once was I able to have a father come in and help. His appearance was so successful I was sorry more fathers were not available.

In addition to the parents of children in your class,

your school can perhaps set up a program for mothers who want to give a definite amount of time on a regular basis, say one or two mornings a week. In schools I have worked in, these volunteers helped out in the library, worked with special teachers in reading, learning disabilities, and art, and assisted in classrooms.

If your school has the opportunity to get student teachers from nearby colleges, by all means volunteer to have one in your room. Along with a teacher aide, a student teacher is the single most valuable resource a teacher can have. Since these students are preparing to be teachers, they can be given a great deal of responsibility in working with small groups of children and will go a long way towards increasing the amount of attention each individual child receives. Because they are students and enthusiastic, they are often full of creative ideas and eager to try them out. A number of ideas in this book originated with former student teachers of mine.

With a student teacher who is just beginning to work in your room, it is best to start by assigning her a very specific task: perhaps giving her a list of four or five children who need help in learning to write their name and suggesting a technique to use in practicing it, such as tracing the name, writing it in sand, or painting it with water on the chalkboard. As the student teacher gains confidence and experience, you should give her more latitude by suggesting the area needing work and letting her devise a way to work on it with the children. At a still later stage, she can use her own judgment to decide which children she would like to work with and what she will do with them.

When you have parent volunteers coming in, you will want to have a specific assignment for them to do. It is probably best that this does not involve academic work as such, but you are the best judge of that. In any case, be sure that all materials necessary for the project are assembled and ready for the volunteer when she arrives. If you will not have time to speak with her ahead of time, it is helpful to have a brief description of the project written on a three-by-five card for her to refer to. These can be kept filed away in a small file box and used over and over again.

Of course, whenever volunteers are involved, there will be difficult times: times when people don't show up and times when they don't follow through with something in the way you would have liked. You must be flexible, adaptable, patient, and willing to work around the difficulties. The advantages of being able to offer the children a much more varied and interesting program are worth the occasional inconveniences. Another problem in working with volunteers who are only with you occasionally (as opposed to student teachers and aides) is that you usually have no set time to plan with them or explain what you want them to do, except when the children are there and you are busy. Your program will run a lot more smoothly if you can get your volunteers to meet you after the children have gone home, or some other time when you are free, so that you can discuss a particular project, what your objectives are, and what the volunteers' specific role will be. But where that is not possible, you should be ready to drop what you are doing for just a few minutes when the volunteer arrives, so that you can get her started. I think you will find the minor inconveniences are worth it, at least until you have that full-time aide you long for!

Bibliography

- Barnouw, Elsa, and Swan, Arthur, ADVENTURES WITH CHILDREN IN THE EARLY SCHOOL YEARS. New York, Agathon, 1986.

- Bott, R. et al, THE TEACHING OF YOUNG CHILDREN: SOME APPLICATIONS OF PIAGET'S LEARNING THEORY, New York, Schocken, 1969.

- Caplan, Frank and Theresa. THE POWER OF PLAY, New York, Doubleday, 1974.

- Hawkins, Frances, THE LOGIC OF ACTION: YOUNG CHILDREN AT WORK, New York, Random House, 1974.

- Holt, John, HOW CHILDREN LEARN, rev. ed., New York, Delacorte, 1983.

- Isaacs, Susan, INTELLECTUAL GROWTH IN YOUNG CHILDREN, New York, Schocken, 1966.

- Spodek, Bernard, TEACHING IN THE EARLY YEARS, 3rd ed., Englewood Cliffs, N.J., Prentice-Hall, 1985.

- Weikart, David, *et al*, THE COGNITIVELY ORIENTED CURRICULUM: A FRAMEWORK FOR PRESCHOOL TEACHERS, Washington, D.C., National Association for the Education of Young Children, 1971.

2

reading readiness

The range of skills that come under the heading of reading readiness at the kindergarten level is wide, encompassing auditory discrimination, auditory memory, visual discrimination, knowledge of the letters of the alphabet, sequencing memory, comprehension, and listening skills. In any kindergarten class, even one that is supposedly homogeneously grouped, you will find children at all stages of development along a continuum. Your job is to find out where each child stands along this continuum, and then to help him master the skills he has not yet acquired as he becomes ready to learn them.

Let me say a word about readiness, since it appears so often in any discussion of a kindergarten program. The range of ages in any given classroom is usually at least a year. Some children may enter at four years eight months, others at five years, others at five years eight months. No one would expect all these children to exhibit the same physical development—to get their permanent teeth at the same time, to be a certain height or weight at the same time—but many parents and teachers become very upset when the younger children do not learn to tie their shoes or write their names or recognize the letters of the alphabet when the others do. It is even worse if the child is older than some other children and has not learned what they have learned. Children's mental growth is as varied as their physical development. No two children even in a single family are toilet-trained in exactly the same way at the same time. By the same token, we should not expect two children, or twenty children, to learn the sound of the letter *b* at the same time.

It has been demonstrated to me repeatedly in working with young children that when a child is ready to learn a particular skill, little actual teaching is needed. We waste a great deal of effort trying to get a concept across to a child before his physical and mental capabilities are developed to the point where he can absorb the concept. Teach him what he needs to know and the job will be much easier. "To delay learning a skill until it is learned easily and with enthusiasm is always good psychology."[1]

Many parents will urge you to begin teaching their child to read "because he wants to learn to read so badly." Of course this is true, since the child observes older brothers and sisters and friends reading, but as Dolch points out many children most emphatically do not want to *work* to learn to read. It is not because they are lazy, but because they have not yet reached the point where they can concentrate all their faculties on the task of learning to read.

Many purely physiological factors are involved. There may be visual problems—crossed eyes, astigmatism, nearsightedness, and others. Also, reading requires accuracy of binocular vision and coordinated eye movements, which may not develop in some children before the eighth year.[2] To begin trying to learn to read before visual coordination is developed places a terrible strain on a child. Children under that strain are easily spotted. When they look at a page or perform other close eye movements, their eyes do not automatically track from left to right. They often have difficulty keeping their place when moving along a row of printed or written lines. (An unfortunate example of the failure to take that into account occurs in the teacher's manual for one widely used reading series. The manual suggests that the first grade teacher give a child a marker if he is having difficulty keeping his eyes on a row of print, instead of pointing out that the child's eye muscles may not yet have developed adequately to perform the task required of them.)

In addition, a child needs to develop the ability to sit

[1]Edward W. Dolch, PSYCHOLOGY AND THE TEACHING OF READ-ING, Westport, Conn., Greenwood Press, 1951, p. 61.

[2]Miles A. Tinker and Constance M. McCullough, TEACHING ELEMEN-TARY READING, New York, Appleton-Century Crofts, 1968.

quietly for a period of time and concentrate on a task. Except for the child who suffers from learning problems or from some emotional disturbance, concentration will develop naturally as the child matures. The child who fidgets and cannot focus his attention for more than a few minutes at a time will benefit greatly if understanding teachers and parents allow him to grow and develop further before he undertakes the task of learning to read. This is true even though other signs of reading readiness, such as the ability to identify letter signs or to recognize some words, may be present.

A child who cannot pick out his own name from among several others is not ready to see the difference between *cat* and *come*. Similarly, if he cannot hear that *day* and *way* sound almost the same, he is not ready to tackle final consonants. In any class of kindergarten children, some will need help in learning to write their names, while others may already be writing their own stories; some children will be able to match words in sentences, while others still have difficulty doing simple wooden puzzles. In a class of first grade children, some may be reading at the start of the year, while others will need help in developing skills, perhaps for nearly a year before they are ready to begin a formal reading program in a pre-primer.

A kindergarten teacher is not generally required to teach reading to all children, as a first grade teacher is. But in many communities, there is great parental pressure to introduce pre-primers as soon as a child shows any signs of ability in one area or another. Both kindergarten and first grade teachers must resist such pressure and allow the children in their classrooms to progress at their own rate.

My own experience has been that children who are really ready to read in kindergarten *do* learn to read, but they learn by themselves, and it is an exciting process for all concerned. One year in the spring we were handing out notices to be sent home to parents. One boy took his paper and began silently sounding out each word, slowly and carefully. Until that point, he had shown interest in various pre-reading activities, but had given no evidence of being able to read. My student teacher called my attention to him and asked:

"Kenny, are you reading?" His reply was, "I don't know, I think so!" and the gradually dawning wonder on his face would have convinced anyone who saw it that children should be allowed to progress at their own pace.

This does not mean that you sit idly by and wait for the magic to happen. Many skills among those described in this chapter can be developed to help the child on his way. As long as he remains interested in the work he does with you and you gear it to his developmental level, you can give him an excellent background even though he may not be ready to begin formal reading instruction for some time. This chapter attempts to help you give appropriate guidance to children at many different levels of development.

Making the Initial Inventory of Skills

During the first weeks of the year, as you are getting to know your students and are beginning to work with them individually or in small groups, spend time with each one to determine roughly what skills he has and where you should begin to help him. Make an inventory of his abilities, including his skill in alphabet recognition, ability to hear rhymes, visual discrimination, and following simple directions. You may wish to include some math topics as well. Your observation of the child during this time will also give you some feeling about his general readiness. If a prekindergarten screening has been held, kindergarten teachers may already have an indication of children who will need help with eye-hand coordination and visual perception.

The following topics are suggestions for inclusion in a first inventory.

Left to Right Progression

As you observe the child at various tasks, see if his eyes generally track from left to right. Does he have difficulty keeping his place? Does he occasionally work from right to left?

Visual Discrimination

Here you want to find out if the child can distinguish between letters that are different (such as *w, c, l*), letters that are quite similar (such as *b, d, p*), words that are quite different (*cat, funny, bear*), and words that are quite similar (*house . . . horse, want . . . went*). Continental Press offers numerous ditto-masters that can be used to test visual discrimination; you can also use workbook pages. In either case, the pages can be mounted on cardboard and covered with clear plastic adhesive. Then they can be marked with a crayon and wiped clean again. The more difficult discriminations should be presented to the child only if he can do the simpler ones with ease.

Alphabet Recognition

You can use flash cards that you hold up and ask the child to name the letter he sees. You may wish to check both capital and lowercase recognition now or defer the lowercase identification to a later time.

Rhyming Words

Tell the child that you are going to say two words that rhyme—that sound almost the same. Then ask him if he can tell you another word that rhymes with them. For example, you say *fan . . . can* and the child supplies *man* or *Dan*. If a child cannot do it at first , try another combination. If he does not seem to know what you are talking about after several examples, stop the test. During the inventory, you never want the child to feel that he has failed because he cannot do something you asked him to do, especially since he will not know you very well at this point. Keep your manner very casual and low key, praise him for his successes and try to find something he can do at each session.

Recognition of Name

If several names of children in the class are laid out on the table, can the child pick out his own name? Many children at the beginning of the year can find names which start with the same letter as theirs, but cannot tell Donald from David, for example.

Writing Name

Can the child write his own name?

Discrimination of Sounds

To find out if a child has developed auditory discrimination to the point where he can hear the different sounds in words, test him by offering him a series of paired words; in some pairs the words will be identical, and in others the words will be similar but not identical. If they are identical, the child is to nod yes, they sound the same. If they are different, he is to tell you no, they are not the same. Ten pairs should be enough to determine his ability to tell the difference, but you may wish to include a few extras if you are not sure.

cat	. . . sat	sat	. . . sat
Don	. . . Don	big	. . . bit
Sup	. . . pup	ten	. . . tan
hot	. . . hot	get	. . . get
shod	. . . shot	tire	. . . tore

NOTE: This test should be given at some time other than immediately before or after the rhyming test, so that the child does not confuse the two tests.

Recognition of Numerals 1 to 10

This may be checked by flash cards.

Counting from One to Ten

Have an assortment of objects (buttons, marbles, candies) in a box. After the child has counted by rote to ten, ask him to give you six marbles, four buttons, three M & M's. You might want to see if he can give you one more than he has, take two from his pile, and so forth.

Identification of Colors and Geometric Shapes

Prepare a set of triangles in different sizes cut from blue construction paper, a set of red circles in different sizes, a set of green rectangles, a set of yellow squares, and so forth, until you have as many colors represented as you wish. (These sets can be used for many different activities other than the inventory, so it is well worth the time needed to prepare them.) Spread a section of shapes and colors on the table and ask the child to pick up the big green circle, the small red circle, the larger blue triangle, and so on, until you have a feeling for his grasp of color, shape, and the concept of big and little.

The inventory will take a period of several weeks to complete. It will take several sessions with each child as you do not wish to tire or frustrate him. But you will find the time spent worthwhile, because it will help you immensely in getting to know the children and determining their level of development before proceeding with a curriculum.

As you are taking the inventory, some questions that you may wish to pose to yourself are: Does the child have a limited vocabulary? Are his sentences complex or is he limited to one-word responses? Does he approach challenge confidently, or is he hesitant and in need of reassurance? Is he able to concentrate on the task at hand for a reasonable period of time? Does he seem to perceive cause-and-effect relationships? Can he group things and ideas in categories easily? Does he remember things? Is he well coordinated physically, on the playground and other areas where you can observe gross-motor movements? How is his fine-motor coordination? Can he hold a pencil easily, catch a ball, and so forth? You might wish to include in the inventory one or two of these simple tests to determine the child's skill in hand movements:

How many blocks high can he build a tower of one-inch cubes? Record the number of cubes just before the tower falls. Record the best of two trials.

How rapidly can he do a simple chore such as putting a number of blocks into a box that just fits them? Scatter the blocks in random style and time the child from the instant he touches the first block until he places the last one. Record the time in seconds. [3]

As he performs various tasks during the inventory, note which hand he habitually uses (in reaching for a pencil, picking out a block, and so forth.)

It will be useful to have a form reproduced to record your findings. You would need one of these for each student. On the next page is a sample of a form to use for kindergarten children. To use it with first grade children, you might want to combine the alphabet recognition with identification of initial consonant sounds. It would also be useful to prepare a list of words from the pre-primers in the reading series you will be using along with other words that might be in a child's sight vocabulary. When you find children who perform many of the inventory tasks with ease, you can check their ability to recognize words on that list.

After the Inventory

At this point a rough division and organization can be made. Folders are made up for various skill areas, and the names of children who are working in these areas are clipped to the front. Some of these topics might be alphabet recognition, rhyming, initial consonants, and small-muscle development. As you work with the children, individually or in small groups, you will get more of a feel for their particular learning needs. The children who are working on rhyming may be subdivided into groups of those who have mastered this particular skill and are ready for another, those who basically have the concept but need reinforcement, and those who are unable to grasp the concept at the time and need more basic help in auditory discrimination.

The work that is done with the children does not mean

[3]Marion Monroé and Bernice Rogers, FOUNDATIONS FOR READING: INFORMAL PRE-READING PROCEDURES, Glenview, Ill., Scott, Foresman, 1964, p. 44.

a daily session in which you take each child one at a time and give him a five- to ten-minute drill or ditto work in the area of his need. At times, you will take a group of children or perhaps one child and direct an activity relating to rhyming, for example, or counting. At other times, children will be choosing activities for themselves that will reinforce a particular skill. Many activities that are games can be devised for children to play on their own with other children or with the help of an aide, a student teacher, a volunteer from another grade level, or a parent. Examples of games on various skills will be included in the sections to follow. In addition, if you organize your classroom around a subject unit, many activities appropriate to the unit will also provide opportunities for the child to increase his competence in a particular skill.

Initial Inventory

NAME _____ DATE COMPLETED _____

Left to right progression	Visual discrimination
Alphabet recognition A B C D E F G H I J K L M N O P Q R S T U V W X Y Z	Rhyming words
Recognizes name	Writes name
Recognizes numerals 1–10	Auditory discrimination
Counts 1–10	
Recognizes basic colors and shapes	Fine-motor skill
Handedness	

General comments and observations

Auditory Discrimination: Initial Skills

In order to help children who are not yet ready for the finer discrimination involved in rhyming words or initial consonants, the games and activities described below may be useful. In fact, children whose auditory skills are more advanced will still enjoy many of these activities.

Encourage musical activities. Using rhythm instruments, beating out rhythmic patterns, listening for high and low sounds, imitating tones and melodies on melody bells, and picking out tunes on the piano are all enjoyable and helpful.

Working in a quiet place with a few children at a time, let them try to guess the origins of some of the following sounds. You can stand behind a screen to produce the sounds, or tape-record them ahead of time and play the tape to the children.

tearing paper	writing on the blackboard
clapping hands	closing a book
jingling money	tearing a piece of cloth
pouring water	cutting with scissors
ringing a bell	winding a clock or a toy
shaking a rattle	snapping a rubber band
closing a zipper	continuing running a record
striking a match	player needle after the
	record is over

Games involving auditory discrimination include:

Who Am I?

One child hides his eyes. Another child is silently picked to come up and stand behind him. In the simplest version, the child asks "Who am I?" in his normal voice and the other child may try three times to guess who it is. A more difficult version allows the child to disguise his voice when he asks the question.

Mother Cat and Her Kittens

Three kittens and a mother cat are chosen. They all lie down to take a nap. While the mother is sleeping the three kittens run and hide. When the mother gets up, she calls the kittens by mewing. She finds them by listening for their answering mews.

Hide the Thimble

One child is chosen to go out of the room while a small object such as a thimble is hidden. When he returns and begins to look for it, the other children help him by clapping louder as he gets closer and softer as he moves away.

Ring Bell Ring

One child hides his eyes while a second child takes a bell to another part of the room. Without looking, the first child says "Ring bell ring" and then points to where he heard the sound coming from.

And there is always Simon Says.

In addition to games such as these, the record player with a listening station encourages children to listen to music and stories. A tape recorder can also be used with a listening station. You can make tapes of familiar sounds for the children to listen to and identify on their own—for example, record the sound of a car starting up, a police siren, a vacuum cleaner, an airplane. Record companies offer sound-effects recordings of a wide variety of natural and mechanical sounds, which children enjoy listening to. Scott, Foresman makes a record set called *Sounds We Hear*, which enables children to identify many common sounds.

Rhyming

Children enjoy listening to rhyming stories and poems, which give them a good introduction to the concept of rhyme. When the stories are familiar, the children can fill in the last words of the line if you pause before completing a sentence. Nursery rhymes can be dramatized either as an activity of the whole class or in small groups. "Humpty Dumpty," "Jack and Jill," and others can be acted out quickly with a minimum of preparation and provide a good introduction to more elaborate dramatizations.

Small groups of children can match pictures of objects that rhyme. The pairs can be laid out on a carpet or a table. Pictures can be cut from magazines, or you can make simple line drawings yourself.

Rhyming lotto cards can be made by pasting or drawing pictures of four words that rhyme on each card. By drawing from a box of individual pictures, children try to cover their card.

Ideal School Supply Company makes a set of Rhyming Objects, a collection of pairs such as a car and a star, a spoon and a moon. Children enjoy handling the objects and they can use them independently or with guidance.

Children can draw pictures to answer riddles in rhyme:

It rhymes with hope.
You use it to wash your hands.

It rhymes with kittens.
When it's cold, you wear them
on your hands.

It rhymes with sled.
You sleep in it.

Have several children sit in a circle with you. Tell them to listen to the pairs of words you say. If the words rhyme, they are to stand up (or clap their hands or put their hands on their heads, etc.).

Pairs of rhyming pictures can be mounted on an electric board, which you can make yourself (see the chapter on making things). When the child correctly matches words that rhyme, a light goes on or a buzzer sounds.

Rhyming pictures can also be set up on a pegboard, with five to ten pictures mounted across one row with hooks beneath. From a selection of pictures, children choose the rhyming ones and hang them underneath each picture.

If a child is able to supply a word to rhyme with a given word, he has a good grasp of the concept of rhyme. Try him on six or seven words: *funny, house, gate, book,* etc. If he cannot immediately think of a rhyming word, he may supply a meaningless syllable, e.g., car . . . sar. See if he can give you another rhyme that is a real word. You may find children using initial consonant substitution as they mentally flip through the possibilities until they find a word they recognize. At this point, they are really isolating the initial consonant sound and are ready for another level of difficulty.

Initial Consonants

Once a child demonstrates an ability to identify and supply rhyming words and an interest in sounds and letters, he can move on to initial consonants.[4] You might start with the letter *f, m,* or *s.* (The letter *b,* often used as an introduction to initial consonants, is actually one of the more difficult ones to isolate. You cannot draw out and exaggerate the sound without distorting it.) Show the child pictures of things that begin with *f.* Let him handle objects whose names begin with *f:* feather, fish, face, fan. Then move on to activities where he must differentiate between objects whose names begin with *f* and those that don't. Some children grasp the concept very quickly and readily acquire the ability to distinguish many letter sounds. Of the ones who do not grasp it immediately, some are obviously ready to learn but need more help, while others simply are not yet ready, although they may have mastered the preceding steps. If a child is ready to learn initial consonants, I have found that even though he may have difficulty learning the first few sounds you go over with him, you begin to see a snowball effect develop, and subsequent sounds are learned much more rapidly. For this reason it is not

[4] Not all children follow this pattern, of course. Some learn initial consonants easily and still do not grasp the concept of rhyme. But in general, it is easier for children to hear similarities in rhyming words than it is to listen for only the difference that the first letter makes, and to isolate that sound. That is why rhyming is usually grasped before initial consonants.

necessary to wait until a child has absolute mastery of one sound before moving on to the next.

Many board games can be adapted for use with initial consonants. Using small pictures of various objects, many of which begin with a particular sound such as *f*, the children draw cards one at a time and can move their markers along the board only when they draw a picture that begins with *f*.

A simple lotto game can be made by ruling square pieces of cardboard or oaktag into nine smaller squares. A key picture is pasted in the center square. Each board you make can have a different initial consonant picture (monkey, fish, bear, etc.) To play, two, three, or four children take a card and then by drawing from a pile of smaller pictures, try to fill their card only with pictures beginning with the same sound as the key picture.

If you have a pegboard in the room, it can be set up so that children match pictures of words that begin the same way (putting pictures of fish, feather and fan beneath a picture of a frog.) Or you can hang up the letters themselves and have the children hang pictures that begin with each letter underneath. If you have an electric board, similar activities can be set up there.

A plastic shoebag with pockets may be used for many sorting activities. Have the children bring in small objects—toy animals, doll furniture, model cars. These can be sorted according to the letter they start with and put in the appropriate pocket of the shoebag (labeled either with a picture or a letter.) Or you can collect a set of coffee cans, label each one with a large letter, and the children can sort the toys as they are brought in.

Old workbooks can be cut up to provide many pictures of words beginning with the common initial consonants. (Houghton Mifflin's readiness book, *Getting Ready to Read*, is particularly good for this.)

Also, keep an alphabetical file of pictures from magazines, Sears Roebuck catalogs, or trading stamp catalogs. When a child is learning about *f*, he can choose four pictures of words that begin with *f* from a variety of pictures on the table. These are pasted in a book, one to a page, and he is encouraged to print the word as the teacher spells it. Once the children have acquired some knowledge of sounds, they enjoy helping to spell the word. Draw out the sounds that they can supply the letter for and let them discover that they can almost spell the word for themselves.

Another approach is to make riddle books or pictures. The child guesses the answer to a riddle such as, "It begins with *f*, it is hot, and it can burn you." and draws a picture of fire on his paper. If a child has a great deal of trouble with printing you can do it for him, but it is best for him to experience the whole association of sound, letter, and meaning as he prints the word himself.

Sometimes a group project is fun. When several children were learning the sound of *d*, we drew a big dinosaur on brown wrapping paper, cut it out and put it on a table with a pile of old magazines, scissors and paste. I told the children the dinosaur was very hungry but he could only eat things that began with *d*. They tried to fill it up by cutting out pictures and pasting over its outline. One child who had a good knowledge of sounds stayed at the table to help the others decide if the pictures they used all started with *d*.

Advanced Auditory Skills

For the children who learn initial consonants early in the year, or who know them when they come to school, you will need to provide more advanced learning experiences. I have found that spelling and working with sounds of words is a very good way to help these children develop their skills. Begin with word-families, by spelling rhyming words. You spell *cat*, then ask the child to spell other words as you pronounce them (*rat, hat, sat,* etc.). As you work with the child to develop the principle—some of course catch on right away while others need more step by step help in sounding out the word—you can show the child the following chart.

Ask him to read the word he will make if he writes *B* in the first space, *S* in the second space, and so forth.

(b)at	ad	un
(s)at	ad	un
(f)at	ad	un

It is possible to devise a movable strip with letters on it that will form different words as it is pulled through a card. If you provide the materials, the child can make his own to take home.

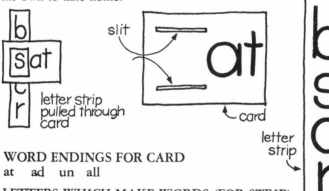

slit

letter strip
pulled through
card

card

letter
strip

WORD ENDINGS FOR CARD
at   ad   un   all

LETTERS WHICH MAKE WORDS (FOR STRIP)
b   c   f   h   m   p   r   s
b   d   h   l   m   p   s
b   f   g   n   r   s
b   c   f   h   t   w

For another activity, children can combine beginnings and endings of words in this table to form whole words and then read them.

	at	it	am
h	hat		
p		pit	
m			

A Word Wheel

can be made from a small paper plate. If the plate has a diameter of eight inches, cut an oaktag circle with a six-inch diameter. Write initial consonants around the edge of smaller circle. The word endings go around the rim of the plate. The oaktag circle is fastened loosely to the plate so it can spin.

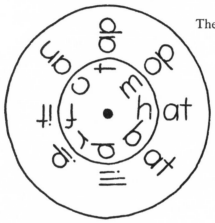

The center marker can be replaced with other letters or even blends.

Word Dice

Use three wooden cubes. On each face of one, print the following letters: **F D P T S B**. On the second print **L H M T C N** and on the third, print **A E I O U E**. Children take turns tossing the dice and try to spell a word with the letters they turn up.

Word Rummy

Oaktag cards the size of playing cards or slightly larger are made with the following letters, one on each card: **B P T S M R L C F D G H K N**. Make three cards for each of the vowels. Children are dealt six cards. They take turns selecting a card from the remaining pile. Each child tries to make a word with the letters in his hand. He discards a card each time he draws one. The first player to use all his cards to make words is the winner.

You will find that some children are learning initial

consonants in September, others in January, others in May, and some will not be ready until after they leave your room. But the exposure to phonics is very beneficial to kindergarten children even when they are not yet ready to learn to read. In fact, I have seen many children who come to reading through writing their own little messages and stories which they were able to create because they knew about the sounds that letters make.

Visual Discrimination

Visual discrimination is an extremely important skill which must be developed before a child can learn to read. No matter what the child's level is, the primary room will provide many challenging and interesting activities to help him grow more skillful in this regard. In addition to puzzles and games you may already have in your classroom, you can make games which will require various degrees of skill in discriminating between shapes, between letters, and between words. The chapter on making things offers directions for making a number of games of this type.

Before a child is ready to see differences between different letters, and from there to see differences between words, he must be able to distinguish between objects that are similar in size, color, or shape. Wooden puzzles provide good practice in this discrimination, as do large wooden beads, wooden building-blocks, flannel shapes to use on a flannel board, and teacher-made lotto games. You may wish to take pages from certain reading readiness workbooks, coat them with clear adhesive paper, and make them available for the children to use. After they have been marked they can be wiped off to use again. Such pages typically show a row of objects: sometimes the objects are the same except in one picture where a crucial detail is missing; sometimes there are three identical objects and one that is different; sometimes only two objects in a row match and the child must pick out the two. A range of difficulty can be provided by selecting different pages from several books. A list of workbooks which contain material of this type can be found in the bibliography.

In order to develop the ability to recognize the letters of the alphabet, some of the following activities may be useful.

Alphabet Lotto

A nine-inch square of cardboard is ruled off into three-inch squares. A capital letter is printed in each square. Several of these boards are made up, each having a different assortment of letters. Three-inch squares of cardboard are made up, each having a capital letter printed on it. These squares are placed face down in a box. One child or several may take a board and choose squares until he fills up his board. Note that the game requires only visual matching of letters. It does not require that the child know the name of the letters.

The same equipment can be used to play ALPHABET BINGO. The child or adult who is caller may either say the name of the letter he draws without showing it to the children (so that they must recognize the letter in order to cover the letter on their card) or say the name of the letter and show it at the same time. This allows children who do not yet know the letters to play.

Go Fish

Make a set of oaktag cards with capital letters printed on them. Seven letters can be used and there should be at least five copies of each one. Several children are dealt four cards each. The rest are placed in the fish pile. Each child in turn asks one of the older children "Do you have any *F*'s?" or whatever letter he chooses. If he gets what he asks for, he can ask again. If not, he draws from the fish pile. Every time someone gets four of a kind, he can lay them down. The first one to get rid of all his cards wins.

If you have a pegboard, hang capital letters on pegs with empty pegs underneath. Provide a tray of similar letters for the children to match by hanging under the correct letter. This can also be done to match capital and lowercase letters, and it, too, could be set up on the electric board.

Children may also form letters out of clay, play with wooden letters, and feel sandpaper letters. They can make their own set of letters to feel by painting the outline of the letters with the clear nail polish and sprinkling sand or salt over the outline before it dries.

Children may be given a sheet of paper with the first letter of their name printed on it and an assortment of gummed squares with which to cover the outline of the letter. This makes a good activity for the first weeks of school.

Many children in kindergarten and first grade have a repertoire of sight vocabulary, or words that they recognize, which is not often used. Words such as stop, exit, cornflakes, coffee, and others that are part of the child's everyday environment are familiar to him. One of the first signs that a child may be on the verge of reading is when he begins to display an active interest in these words, asking what they say, spelling them, and remembering them. But even before a child is ready to read, he can become interested in words when they become a part of new and interesting experiences.

Using whatever skill in visual discrimination he has acquired, plus aids such as picture clues and memory associations, children can learn to recognize a number of words. The more advanced child will make these words a part of his sight vocabulary; he will be able to recognize them in new contexts even without the clues that originally helped him to know the words. Other children will continue to need to see the word in its original context—*RED* on a color chart with a bright red piece of paper next to it; *COFFEE* printed on a coffee can—and can "read" the word there but not in an unfamiliar context. (I place the word "read" in quotation marks here and in other places to indicate that the child is using any of a variety of clues to recognize isolated words. While he is not reading in the strict sense of the word, he has taken an important beginning step in learning to decode words.)

While the development of a sight vocabulary is one of the more advanced skills in the area of visual discrimination, even children whose skills are at a less advanced point will benefit by many of the experiences described below. Children of kindergarten age are naturally fascinated with words and letters and respond eagerly to activities that they can see are a prelude to reading.

The children can make simple books with only one word to a page, accompanied by a picture or their own drawing of the thing named. These they will be able to "read" for themselves with great pride. The initial consonant books previously mentioned are one example, and other possibilities will be suggested by the unit being studied in the room. If you are learning about Indians, for example, you can put out on a table six or eight simple pictures of Indian objects: a totem pole, a drum, a tom-tom, a papoose. Label the pictures in capital letters. (If many of your children can print lowercase letters easily, you can label the pictures that way. Or provide labels in both lower case and capitals so that children can choose the one they feel most comfortable with.) After the child has made drawings of several Indian objects and copied the names underneath, the pages can be stapled together and given a cover and a title. At Christmastime, pictures of holiday symbols can be put out with labels: a star, a candle, a candy cane, a menorah (for Hanukkah). Other books of this type can be made about Halloween, seashore creatures, animals, rocket ships, and the circus. Because the words are familiar and the pictures offer a clue, children keep these books and "read" them many times to themselves, to other children and to their families.

Don't neglect the finishing touches, such as an attractive book cover and carefully printed title, for all these books that the children make. If your supply of construction paper is limited, get old wallpaper books and use the pages for book covers. This final step is extremely important to the child; it makes the difference between a book that has some resemblance to the ones on bookshelves and something which is just a few sheets of paper carelessly fastened together because the teacher was too busy to do anything better.

Labeling provides an opportunity for children to learn to recognize many words because of their association with familiar objects. Print signs for objects in the room on oaktag strips and tape them in place: blackboard, piano, sink, door, window, flag. After the children have become quite familiar with these words, without saying anything to them ahead of time, switch the labels around one day before the children arrive.

See how many children notice immediately that something is wrong! A student teacher in my room added interest to this activity by bringing in three baseball caps, pinning a *D* on each one for Detective, and providing three clipboards and pencils. The children were invited to take a hat and a clipboard and go around the room writing down the words that were in the wrong place. This was one of our most popular activities for several weeks, even among children who could barely hold a pencil and who showed little interest in writing under other circumstances.

A variation of this activity that also proved popular called for matching words to words. I made a set of picture cards with the words printed underneath. Simple, large magazine pictures of a truck, a lion, a typewriter, a car, an apple, shoes, and other things were used. Another set of cards was made that had only the printed word. The pictures were tacked all over the room, high and low. I would give a child three or four word cards and ask him to find the pictures with words that matched his cards. Often children whose visual discrimination was not yet up to whole words would work with another child who could match more easily. The activity was entirely voluntary, but it was unusual to find cards lying unused on the table.

Word charts can be made for various subjects. Colored squares with the names of the color printed next to them, or a list of numerals with their names printed next to them can be displayed on a bulletin board. Once the children have become somewhat familiar with them, color words and pieces of colored paper can be mounted on an electric board or pegboard so that children can try to match the word with the correct color. As each new unit gets under way, many new words will be discussed, and these can be presented on similar charts. Indian words, holiday words, names of pets, kinds of food, parts of the body: all will be interesting to the children because of the context.

For children who are actually about to read, all the activities described above will not only create an interest in words but will help develop a sight vocabulary. As children begin to learn to read, a growing vocabulary is as important as a developing skill in phonics.

A beginning reader who relies only on sounding out each word will be reading very laboriously, and besides, many common words do not correspond to phonics rules. On the other hand, though, mere memorization of a sight vocabulary will propel him only through the simplest pre-primers. Both approaches should be used: teach the child how to decode the printed symbols, and help him to develop a vocabulary of familiar words that he recognizes right away.

Reading vocabulary can be developed through the use of word books or files. A picture dictionary can be started in a spiral notebook. The child can cut out or draw pictures and print the words underneath. The book can be organized in alphabetical order or according to subject. In the same way that Sylvia Ashton-Warner worked with her pupils in New Zealand,[5] you can supply the child with words he wants to know, and he can print them on slips of paper and keep them in his own box. Children should be encouraged to write as much as possible, both for self-expression and to give them their own material to read. In most cases this will be done by dictating the stories to an adult or older child, but every now and then you will find children who begin to write out simple sentences on their own.

Comprehension

If a child is not able to understand what he reads and then to remember it, it does not matter how competent he is at decoding words, as any harassed teacher of upper-grade children will gladly tell you. As a kindergarten teacher, there are several ways in which you can help the child lay the foundation for the acquisition of the important skills of comprehension and memory.

Perhaps the single most important way to help children learn to comprehend what they hear and later what they read is to read stories aloud to them. Reading

[5]Sylvia Ashton-Warner, TEACHER, New York, Simon & Schuster, 1963, 1971 (paper) and Bantam, 1971 (paper).

stories is thus an extremely important part of every kindergarten program. Each day, as you read a story, pause occasionally to ask the children what they think will happen next. This encourages careful listening and good reasoning, and it also helps to increase the suspense. As you finish the story, ask the children one or two questions about what happened. Sometimes the questions can merely test recollection: Whom did Little Red Riding Hood meet in the forest? and sometimes they can be interpretive: Why do you think Little Red Riding Hood didn't do what her mother told her to?

Developing an understanding of sequence, of how one thing follows another in a story, will aid the children in remembering and understanding, and also will help them as they begin to write more complex stories of their own. One way to develop an understanding of sequence is to stage dramatizations of stories in the classroom. Planning the dramatizations provides a good opportunity for children to think about the sequence of events, since they will need to plan which scene to act when, how many characters are needed, and so forth. In addition to nursery rhymes, which are easy to do since they are so short and are familiar to most children, the following stories are all excellent for dramatizing: "Three Little Pigs," "Little Red Riding Hood," "Three Billy Goats Gruff," "Hansel and Gretel," "The Gingerbread Man," and "Caps For Sale."

Use a flannel board to encourage retelling of a story. Either make cutouts or have children draw the characters, cut them out, and then mount them on stiff paper and back them with flannel. If they are made available to the children after you have read the story, you will find children gravitating to the figures, either alone or in small groups, and acting out the story, retelling it for themselves. The value of the activity for developing both language and memory skills and for encouraging group efforts cannot be overemphasized.

Sometimes workbooks or old discarded storybooks will have illustrations of well-known nursery rhymes or stories that you can cut out, mount, and back with flannel. They can be left at the flannel board for children to arrange in sequence. It is best to keep this activity quite simple at first, using no more than three or four pictures, because the ability to arrange things in sequence is a fairly advanced skill. You could make a few more complicated sets of pictures, requiring the ordering of five or more pictures, but do not expect many children to be able to master them.

Children can make puppets of characters in a story and will enjoy using them in an impromptu puppet theatre set up on a desk or large carton, perhaps with a tablecloth for a curtain. Stick puppets are probably the easiest to make. The child draws and cuts out his character and an ice cream stick is mounted on the back. Strips of cardboard can also be used. Paper bag puppets are also fun to make. You provide lunch-size bags, yarn, magic markers, scraps of ribbon, and so forth, and children can go on from there.

A rather elaborate procedure that can be fun is to make a cartoon from a favorite story. Be prepared to spend some time on it and try to plan the work for a time when you will have some help in the room. Any home movie camera can be used, and a tripod is helpful although not absolutely essential. After choosing the story to be filmed, a background must be made. For "Little Red Riding Hood," we took several sheets of twelve-by-eighteen-inch drawing paper and taped them in a row. The background scenes were colored in with magic markers and crayon, starting with Little Red Riding Hood's cottage on the left, then a long section of woods with trees and flowers and a path, and concluding with the grandmother's cottage at the end. We found that a scene of the interior of the grandmother's house was also needed. Then the characters, which the children had drawn, were colored and cut out; they were Red Riding Hood, her mother, her grandmother, the wolf, and the woodsman.

In order to animate a film, very slight alterations in position are photographed for short intervals, perhaps ten seconds at a time. When the film is shown on a screen, these isolated changes are blended so quickly one after the other that they are perceived as movement. To begin your filming, find a level place with plenty of light. Depending on your camera, you may need to film outdoors or you may be able to film indoors with or without floodlights. Fix the camera on the tripod, if you are using one, so that it is the correct distance from the backdrop. If the camera is hand-held, mark your position on the floor with a piece of tape at the correct distance so you can always find the exact spot when you resume filming. Be sure the camera is in focus before you begin shooting.

Have a child place the figures of Little Red Riding Hood and her mother at the door of the cottage. Film the scene for a sufficient length of time to allow the necessary dialogue to be filled in later (you can say the words silently to give yourself an idea of how long it will take.) Then have the child move Little Red Riding Hood very slightly towards the forest just half an inch or so. Film for ten seconds. Have the child move the figure again slightly. You can have the figure tilted slightly to the right and to the left alternately to give more of the appearance of walking, if desired. Continue filming this way until the wolf appears. The children can take turns moving the figures, as it is a very time-consuming process.

The wolf is inserted next to Little Red Riding Hood between filmings. Again, at this point you will want to expose a longer portion of film to allow their conversation to be inserted later. You can pause occasionally to allow the two figures to be moved slightly so they won't appear to be stock-still while they are talking. Now move the wolf slowly along toward the grandmother's house. Show him getting rid of the grandmother, getting into bed, and so forth. Continue filming the story, always being sure to allow enough exposure at points where you will want to fit in dialogue.

After the film is developed, it is possible to tape the story. Let the children watch the film several times and then they can practice retelling the story along with the film. When they have it fairly well synchronized, record the story, and you will have a cartoon with soundtrack for the children to enjoy over and over again.

Creative Writing

One of the most important tools for developing the child's interest in reading and for helping him to improve his skills as he begins to read is to use his own words written down as something to read. For children who are far from being able to read for themselves, hearing their own stories read to the class, or having them attractively prepared for them to take home to their parents, is a tremendously satisfying and ego-building experience. Children who are actually learning to read will also love to hear their stories read, and in addition it will provide them with more meaningful and interesting reading material than the most carefully constructed pre-primer.

The process of seeing their ideas take written form is also extremely important in helping children develop an understanding of the whole process of communication and language. Lee and Allen describe how the whole process begins to make sense to the child when he is given many opportunities to express his thoughts and feelings and see them written down to be read by others:

What I think about I can understand.
What I say I can write.
What I can write I can read.
I can read what I write and other
people can write for me to read. [6]

A good way to begin encouraging the child to express himself is through his art work. Right from the beginning of the year, whenever you ask him about a painting or drawing or other project, take the time to write down his response on a piece of paper and attach it to the picture. Share these picture stories with the whole class—a few minutes every day or so. Even if a child tells you only a few words about his work, it is worthwhile to enable him to see his ideas put down in print and to hear them shared with others. (Of course, these things should never be read to the others without the author's permission.) Encourage helpers who may visit your room to be available for this kind of dictation. Some of the children's most exciting writing will come out of these sessions.

Trips, also, provide a wonderful opportunity to expand children's horizons and to stimulate language develop-

[6]Dorris M. Lee and Richard V. Allen, LEARNING TO READ THROUGH EXPERIENCE, New York, Appleton-Century-Crofts, 1963.

ment through conversation, pictures, and creative stories. Every kindergarten program should include many trips—trips to the pet store to buy fish for the classroom, trips to the firehouse and police station, trips to the grocery store to buy things for a project or party, trips to a nature preserve for an autumn walk, to a cider mill, a post office, a bakery.

After each trip, children can be encouraged to record their impressions in some way. They can draw a picture and tell about what they saw or record their ideas into a tape recorder; the tape may be played back later to the class.

In another exercise, each child can contribute one sentence about what he saw, and the sentences can be written on large oaktag paper and kept up in the room to be read back at a later time. Or, the sentences can be dittoed and made into a book for the children to take home. A book with so many sentences will be too much for the child to read for himself, though he often can read a simple story of one or two sentences that he has written himself. But the children enjoy hearing the book read to them because of its association with their classmates and the trip.

You can take photographs of the trip and when they are developed they can be mounted in book form with the children supplying the descriptions.

Photographs of children involved in various classroom activities such as block building, doll play, and cooking are excellent story-starters. Unfortunately it can be quite expensive to do that on a large scale. If you take black and white snapshots and can develop them yourself or know someone who can, the cost becomes much more reasonable. One year, a high school boy who was very interested in photography came to several kindergarten classes in the school where I worked. He took candid pictures of the children and developed them into eight-by-ten prints. Perhaps you can find a hobbyist who would like to get involved in a similar project.

Keep a file of interesting magazine pictures. Many advertisers use first-rate photographers to take their pictures, and many of the photos are very appealing to children. Put a selection of such pictures out on a table with a primary typewriter near by, and be available for children who want to tell you about a particular picture. Of course, you can print the stories instead of typing them, but if you have access to a typewriter, use it now and then even if you make mistakes. Children are fascinated to see the words form as if by magic on the paper as they say them, and particularly if you use a primer typewriter, the story will be printed the way their early reading books will be.

Prints of abstract art or unusual magazine pictures that are open to widely varying interpretations can be preserved and used over and over again. What do you see in the picture? can be asked of many different children, and all the reactions can be printed out and hung up along with the picture and then discussed.

You can provide the child with a sheet of paper on which a few lines—curved, straight, wavy—are placed at random, and ask him to use the lines to make a picture. When he is finished, the picture can be pasted to one side of a folded piece of twelve-by-eighteen-inch construction paper and his story about the picture can be written opposite. A simple book is the result.

Depending on the time of year or the unit being studied, children can be asked to complete sentences such as the following and illustrate them if desired:

On Halloween I will . . .
If I were an Indian, I would . . .
I had a dream that I . . .
The best thing that could happen is . . .
When I grow up I will . . .
I was scared when . . .

A child can write his own story to accompany the pictures in any one of the several books without words that are in print for children. A list of some of these books is given in the bibliography at the end of this chapter. Removable adhesive labels called Pres-a-ply, put out by Dennison, can be bought at many stationery stores. They come in many sizes, some of which are large enough to accommodate several sentences. A child's version of a story in a book without words can be printed on the labels and pasted in the book; afterward the labels can be removed and another story put in. Be sure to check that the label will peel off easily before completing the book since some materials seem to make the labels adhere more firmly than others.

Blank books containing four to six pages of clean white paper can be stapled together with attractive wallpaper covers and given to the children to make their own stories in. By answering the question, What or whom do you want your story to be about? children can be helped to make the transition from a one page story such as they might tell about a particular drawing to one that is several pages long, although there may be only one or two sentences to a page. They can draw the answer to the question on the first page of the book, and you can write the description. What happens to him? becomes the second page, and so on until the story is finished. This may seem rather mechanical, but I have found that it helps children to get started when they are ready to tell a more complicated kind of sequential story. Once they get the idea, some children really take off, often exhausting willing parents and teachers with their dictations. Children who reach this point are usually able to read their own stories, and often each other's stories, so you will have a ready supply of interesting reading material for them.

Books for Teachers

- Durkin, Dolores, TEACHING YOUNG CHILDREN TO READ, Boston, Allyn and Bacon, 1976.

- Getman, G. N., Kane, E. R., Halgren, M. R., and McKee G. W., THE PHYSIOLOGY OF READINESS, Chicago, Lyons and Carnahan, 1966.

- Harris, Albert J. and Sipay, Edward R., HOW TO INCREASE READING ABILITY, 6th ed. New York, David McKay, 1976.
  See Unit 2, Reading Readiness: What, Why, and How

- Hillerich, Robert L. READING FUNDAMENTALS FOR PRESCHOOL AND PRIMARY CHILDREN, Columbus, Charles E. Merrill, 1977.

- Palewicz-Rousseau, Pam, and Maderas, Lynda, THE ALPHABET CONNECTION: A PARENTS' AND TEACHERS' GUIDE TO BEGINNING READING AND WRITING, New York, Schocken, 1979.

- Lowell, Edgar, and Stoner, Marguerita, PLAY IT BY EAR: AUDITORY TRAINING GAMES, Los Angeles, John Tracy Clinic, 1963.
- Tinker, Miles A., and McCullough, Constance M., TEACHING ELEMENTARY READING, 4th ed. Englewood Cliffs, N.J., Prentice-Hall, 1975.
- Valett, Robert E., THE REMEDIATION OF LEARNING DISABILITIES: A HANDBOOK OF PSYCHOEDUCATIONAL RESOURCE PROGRAMS, Belmont, Calif., Fearon Publishers, 1967.
  This book gives many suggestions for helping the learning-disabled child, which are also extremely useful for other children. Many specific activities in each reading readiness area are given. The bibliography is excellent.

Workbooks Containing Visual Discrimination Exercises

- Allyn and Bacon, MOVING DAYS
- American Book Company, STARTING OFF
- Economy Company, MUD-LUSCIOUS, EARLY LIGHT
- Ginn and Company, READY FOR RAINBOWS
- Harcourt Brace Jovanovich, LOOK, LISTEN, AND LEARN
- Harper and Row, GET READY
- Holt, Rinehart and Winston, ABOUT ME, HEAR, SAY, SEE, AND WRITE
- Houghton Mifflin, GETTING READY TO READ
- Macmillan, STARTING OUT
- Scott, Foresman, HELLO SUNSHINE

Commercial Materials Rhyming

- Instructo

Fun with Rhymes
Rhyming Pictures (for Flannel Board)

Let's Have a Nursery Rhyme Party

- Ideal   Rhyming Puzzles
  Rhyming Chart

  Objects that Rhyme
  Rhyming Pictures for Peg
  Board

- Milton Bradley   Pictures that Rhyme

Visual Discrimination and Alphabet Recognition

- Instructo   Visual Discrimination—
  set of spirit masters
  Three-dimensional visual
  discrimination kit
  Wooden Alphabet Letters
  Kinesthetic Alphabet Cards
  Stepping Stones—Alpha-
  bets, capitals and lowercase

- Milton Bradley   Alphabet puzzle cards
  Alphabet Picture Flash
  Cards

- Kenworthy   ABC game

- Ben-G   Ready-To-Read puzzles

- Creative Play-
  things   Find It/Picture Finding
  Lotto
  Shape Dominoes
  Picture Dominoes
  Face Matching

- Playskool   Alphabet Zoo

- Lauri   Alphabet Avalanche

Initial Consonants

- Instructo   Toy Chest of Beginning
  Sounds (for Flannel Board)

  Carnival of Beginning
  Sounds

- Milton Bradley   Beginning Consonant
  Poster Cards
  Beginning Sounds Flannel
  Aid

■ Ideal	Consonant Pictures for Peg Board
	Magic Cards—Consonants
	Initial and Final Consonant Charts

| ■ McGraw-Hill | Match the Sounds Puzzle |

| ■ Dolch | What the Letters Say |
| | Consonant Lotto |

| ■ Scott, Foresman | Talking Alphabet |

Advanced Phonics

■ St. Regis	Picture Word Matching Game
	Phonics Bingo
	Picture Phonics Cards

| ■ Ideal | Silly Sounds |

| ■ Creative Playthings | Reading Lotto |

| ■ Trend Enterprise | Initial Consonant Bingo |

■ ABC School Supply Co., Atlanta, Georgia	Oxford Picture and Word Making Cards
	Actions Picture and Word Making Cards
	Make-a-Word Spelling Game
	Word Family Phonics

| ■ Instructo | Initial Consonant Substitution |
| | Consonant Combination Puzzles |

| ■ Dolch | Picture Word Cards |

| ■ Milton Bradley | Picture Flash Words for Beginners |

Stories that Rhyme

- Berenstain, Stan and Berenstain, Janice, OLD HAT, NEW HAT, New York, Random House, 1970.

- Burroway, Janet, THE TRUCK ON THE TRACK, Indianapolis, Bobbs-Merrill, 1970.

- Cameron, Polly, THE GREEN MACHINE, New York, Coward, McCann & Geoghegan, 1969.
"I CAN'T" SAID THE ANT, New York, Coward, McCann & Geoghegan, 1961.

- Cole, William, THAT PEST, JONATHAN, New York, Harper & Row, 1970.

- Cox, Palmer, BUGABOO BILL, New York, Farrar, Straus & Giroux, 1971.

- Eichenberg, Fritz, APE IN A CAPE, New York, Harcourt Brace Jovanovich, 1973.
DANCING IN THE MOON: COUNTING RHYMES, New York, Harcourt Brace, 1956.

- Fisher, Aileen, CLEAN AS A WHISTLE, New York, Crowell, 1969.

- Kahl, Virginia, HOW DO YOU HIDE A MONSTER?, New York, Scribner, 1971.

- Kent, Jack, THE GROWN-UP DAY, New York, Parents' Magazine Press, 1969.

- Kraus, Robert, WHOSE MOUSE ARE YOU?, New York, Macmillan, 1970, 1972 (paper).

- Lasson, Robert, WHICH WITCH?, New York, David McKay, 1959.

- MacPherson, Elizabeth H., A TALE OF TAILS, Racine, Wisc., Western Publishing (Golden Press), 1971.

- Ormerod, Jan, RHYMES AROUND THE DAY, New York, Lothrop, Lee and Shepard, 1983.

- Paxton, Tom, JENNIFER'S RABBIT, New York, Putnam, 1970.

- Peet, Bill, THE CABOOSE WHO GOT LOOSE, Boston, Houghton Mifflin, 1971.

- Schurr, Cathleen, CATS HAVE KITTENS, DO GLOVES HAVE MITTENS?, New York, Knopf, 1962.

Alphabet Books

- Anno, Mitsumatsa, ANNO'S ALPHABET, New York, Thomas Y. Crowell, 1975.

- Crews, Donald, WE READ ABC'S, New York, Greenwillow, 1983.

- DeBrunhoff, Laurent, BABAR'S ABC, New York, Random House, 1985.

- Gag, Wanda, ABC BUNNY, New York, Coward, McCann & Geoghegan, 1933.

- Gordon, Isabel, THE ABC HUNT, New York, Viking Press, 1961.

- Greenaway, Kate, A-APPLE PIE, New York, Warne, 1886.

- Ipcar, Dahlov, I LOVE MY ANTEATER WITH AN A, New York, Knopf, 1964.

- Lobel, Arnold and Anita, ON MARKET STREET, New York, Greenwillow, 1981.

- *Miles, Miska, APRICOT ABC, Boston, Little, Brown, 1969.

- Munari, Bruno, BRUNO MUNARI'S ABC, New York, Harper & Row, 1960.

- *Newberry, Clare T., THE KITTENS' ABC, New York, Harper & Row, 1965.

- *Piatti, Celestino, CELESTINO PIATTI'S ANIMAL ABC, New York, Atheneum, 1966.

- Sendak, Maurice, ALLIGATORS ALL AROUND, New York, Harper & Row, 1962.

- Tudor, Tasha, A IS FOR ANNABELLE, New York, Henry Z. Walck, 1954.

- Wildsmith, Brian, BRIAN WILDSMITH'S ABC, New York, Watts, 1963.

Books Without Words

- Alexander, Martha, BOBO'S DREAM, New York, Dial, 1970.

- Anno, Mitsumatsa, ANNO'S JOURNEY, New York, Collins, 1978. ANNO'S USA, New York, Philomel, 1983.

- Ardizzone, Edward, THE WRONG SIDE OF THE BED, New York, Doubleday, 1970.

- Aruego, Jose, LOOK WHAT I CAN DO, New York, Scribner, 1971.

- Baum, Willi, BIRDS OF A FEATHER, Reading, Mass., Addison-Wesley, 1969.

- Carle, Eric, DO YOU WANT TO BE MY FRIEND?, New York, Thomas Y. Crowell, 1971.

- Crews, Donald, TRUCK, New York, Greenwillow, 1980.

- Goodall, John S., PADDY FINDS A JOB, New York, Atheneum, 1981
PADDY GOES TRAVELING, New York, Atheneum, 1982.
SHREWBETINNA GOES TO WORK, New York, Atheneum, 1981.

*These books are written in rhyme.

- Hamberger, John, THE LAZY DOG, New York, Scholastic Book Services (Four Winds Press), 1971.

- Hogrogian, Nonny, APPLES, New York, Macmillan, 1972.

- Hutchins, Pat, CHANGES, CHANGES, New York, Macmillan, 1971.

- Krahn, Fernando, THE CREEPY THING, New York, Clarion, 1982.
  A FLYING SAUCER FULL OF SPAGHETTI, New York, Dutton, 1970.

- Mari, Iela and Mari, Enzo, THE APPLE AND THE MOTH, New York, Pantheon, 1969.
  THE CHICKEN AND THE EGG, New York, Pantheon, 1969.

- Mayer, Mercer, FROG, WHERE ARE YOU?, New York, Dial, 1969.
  A BOY, A DOG, AND A FROG, Eau Claire, Wisc., E. M. Hale, 1972.

- Meyer, Renate, HIDE-AND-SEEK; A PICTURE BOOK, Scarsdale, N.Y., Bradbury Press, 1972.

- Ringi, Kjell, THE WINNER, New York, Harper & Row, 1969.

- Schick, Eleanor, MAKING FRIENDS, New York, Macmillan, 1969.

- Speir, Peter, NOAH'S ARK, New York, Doubleday, 1978.
  PETER SPEIR'S RAIN, New York, Doubleday, 1982.

- Turkle, Brinton, DEEP IN THE FOREST, New York, Dutton, 1976.

- Wezel, Peter, THE GOOD BIRD, New York, Harper & Row, 1964.
  THE NAUGHTY BIRD, Chicago, Ill., Follett, 1967.

3

mathematics

In many kindergarten and first grade classrooms, some sort of math workbook full of attractive colored drawings serves as the basis for the entire math program. The trouble with such an approach is that it often introduces abstractions too quickly and does not allow for the large amounts of manipulative exploration and discovery that are necessary for a firm foundation in mathematical concepts. It is far better for the child at the beginning of his experience with math in school to spend a great deal of time discovering a few basic concepts and developing ideas about fundamental mathematical relationships. With a good foundation, paper and pencil skills will come much more easily later.

Broad basic concepts that need to be developed before further exploration can take place and that are appropriate to the young child are these:

Classifying, grouping, and other set relationships;

Counting, both rote and meaningful, including recognizing number names and symbols, and differentiating between cardinal and ordinal numbers;

Making size and number comparisons, including estimating;

Space relationships; shape, location, symmetry, perspective, and geometric shapes.

You may wonder how you can find time to develop these skills individually in each of your children. Certainly it will take more time than group lessons from a workbook. But many of the activities suggested in this chapter may be done with four or five children at a time, and in fact this group work is often preferable to individual work because children are learning to work together, and they can share their experience in solving problems. Besides, much of the math experience at the beginning level is play-discovery; through manipulating and exploring a wide variety of materials, children will be making discoveries on their own. Your job is to guide and direct the children who are ready for more structured learning and to allow them all plenty of time to experiment and discover.

Certain features of any typical primary classroom already contain the materials for encouraging the development of math concepts. As the children play in the block corner, building towers and buildings, they are constantly dealing with size, shape, weight, height, and number. At the water table, they are learning about capacity as they pour water or soapsuds endlessly from one container to another. At the snack table, they learn about one-to-one correspondence when they ask themselves whether there are enough cookies, whether they need to get more paper cups, whether there is an empty chair for them.

Classification

There are many specific ways you can further develop the basic concepts of mathematics in your classroom. Classification, which includes grouping, ordering sets, and other set relationships, is an important area of concepts that precedes the development of counting skills. Counting is actually a refinement of classifying and ordering objects, since in counting we are giving a very specific order to a group of objects. Classification is also a basic tool of logic: practice in seeing likenesses and differences, perceiving categories, and making judgments based on these perceptions are important aspects of developing powers of thinking.

From the very beginning of his daily life in the classroom, the child makes classifications frequently. He learns that the crayons are put away in this box, wheel toys in that corner, books on the shelf. In the playhouse, children select small clothes for the baby doll and larger clothes for other dolls. When a child borrows a toy from another child, he knows that that toy is returned to that child and not to the classroom set. More sophisticated classifications can be developed in other activities. The child can learn to sort objects by different categories: by shape, by color, by size, by whether they are made of wood, metal, or plastic, by function (things we eat with, things we wear), and by class (animal or plant). Classification can be incorporated into a particular unit of study through the use of pictures as well as objects. In late October, children can sort Halloween candy into baskets for a party or for donation to a children's hospital. If you are studying animals, pictures of animals can be sorted into piles according to whether they swim, fly, or walk, or whether they have fur, feathers, or scales.

The Science Curriculum Improvement Study (SCIS) has as part of a unit on material objects an excellent Button Box activity. Each child is given an assortment of buttons and a small tray or paper plate and asked to sort his buttons as he wishes. Afterwards, the various methods are discussed; some will have been sorted by color, some by shape, some by material, some by size, and some by number of holes in the buttons.

Children can be asked to compare objects by weight (this is heavier, that is lighter) and height (this is taller, that is shorter). Various science experiments provide opportunities for classifying objects. Testing a collection to see which will sink and which will float and which can be picked up by a magnet and which cannot are two examples. The results of these experiments can be recorded by pasting the objects in each category on a piece of heavy paper or cardboard under simple captions. (These did not float.) Or the child can draw pictures on either side of a piece of folded paper and the pictures can be labeled. That enables him to "read" about the results of his work.

Graphing provides a wealth of opportunity for helping young children to classify and order objects. *Teaching Mathematics to Young Children: A Basic Guide,* by Rosalie Jensen and Deborah Spector (Englewood Cliffs, NJ, Prentice-Hall, 1984), has a number of ideas on projects to introduce graphing in the section, "Early Experience Recording Numbers." One way graphs can be used to record classifications is to analyze the class according to one variable or another: How many children are wearing short sleeves and how many are wearing long sleeves? How many are wearing sneakers and how many are wearing regular shoes? How many have blue eyes? green eyes? brown eyes? In the beginning, results should be recorded pictorially. Have all the long-sleeve wearers stand to one side and the short-sleeve wearers to the other. Make a simple graph on the chalkboard using sketches of long-sleeve shirts and short-sleeve shirts to represent the numbers of children in each category. That kind of activity is a good way to begin the day when you have all the children together. It involves all the children, and there is no particular advantage to be gained by doing it in small groups, although many other kinds of graphs can be done individually or in small groups.

Ordering Objects and Patterning

Learning to put objects in a particular order is part of the general category of classifying, but a more advanced step, one that approaches the use of ordinal numbers. Of course, most children come to school with the ability to count by rote, and so they are acquainted with ordinal numbers. But the point of all the preliminary activity is to develop a background of experience with and real understanding of mathematical concepts, rather than simple rote learning. Most kindergarten teachers have had the experience of seeing children who could rattle off the numbers from one to twenty but who could not hand you five crayons or, if you had five in your hand, could not tell you how many you would have if one more were added.

One way to think about ordering objects is to think about pairs of things. The children can list all the things they can think of that come in twos: shoes, earrings, legs, hands, ears, twins, skates. You can talk about objects that go together: cup and saucer, shoes and socks, washer and bolt. In these cases, the order of the object is important: you don't put your shoe on before your sock, and you don't put a cup down and then put a saucer over it. This introduces the principle of commutativity: that certain mathematical statements, such as 2 + 3, can be reversed and still keep their meaning, while others, such as 3 − 2, cannot.

The child can be asked to order a group of objects, such as silverware, according to a certain pattern: knife, fork, and spoon. He can hang cutouts of articles of clothing on a laundry line in the same order that they appear on another laundry line. He can string various shaped and colored beads in a pattern that follows a sample. Arranged in order of difficulty, a series of bead stringing tasks might be:

Make a pattern of red square, yellow square, red square, yellow square (no shape variable, two color variables);

Make a pattern of red square, red circle, red square, red circle (no color variable, two shape variables);

Make a pattern of red circle, green circle, yellow circle (no shape variable, three color variables);

Red circle, yellow square, green circle, yellow square, red circle (both color and shape varied).

A slightly more difficult task is posed by asking the child to work from a picture card of the pattern to be copied rather than from another string of beads. Some fairly complex patterns can be pictured on cards and made available to children who are ready to tackle them. This practice encourages the use of logic and reasoning power, and is a prelude to the development of more advanced concepts. The ability to perceive patterns in what at first appear to be random assortments of things and to predict on the basis of this what the next steps in the chain will be is an important thinking skill which can be developed at an early age.

Patterning can also be incorporated into units of study. For example, during a unit on Indians, headbands can be decorated with cut-out geometric shapes put together in patterns, either from sample cards or from the child's own design. At Christmastime, the classroom tree can be decorated with strings composed of popcorn, cranberries, and macaroni strung according to different patterns.

Graph paper can be used to create patterns that children can copy, and then they can go on to create their own. Paper ruled into one-inch squares is best. If you don't have graph paper, you can make ditto-masters and run off an ample supply. Cut the paper into five-inch squares. Make up some sample patterns by pasting colored one-inch squares in different arrangements on the five-inch papers. Keep them simple at first. As a free-choice activity, children may go to a table where many of these samples are laid out along with blank graph paper squares, many small colored squares, and glue. They choose a pattern to copy and glue the squares on their own paper. A possible variation is to use crayons to color in the squares instead of pasting colored paper. Children enjoy making up their own designs.

Working with a pegboard is another chance for children to make patterns. Start them out by placing a series of colored pegs in a certain sequence in a row and asking them to complete the row using the same sequence of colors (two reds, one green, three yellows, over and over). Children enjoy making patterns for you to follow as well. Or two children can work together to make patterns for each other. In all of this work, encourage left to right progression. I have seen recommendations that children be encouraged to reverse patterns after proficiency is gained, but my own feeling is that with young children, especially those who may not yet be working consistently from left to right, this further refinement can be very confusing and possibly detrimental to the development of an important reading skill.

Patterning can also be developed by working on a large grid on the floor. By marking off a large square three feet by three feet with masking tape, and then dividing it into nine-inch squares, you have an area for children to lay out patterns. Mark out a similar grid for yourself and lay out the colored shapes, blocks, or whatever material you are using in a particular pattern. Leaving your pattern for reference, ask the child to lay out a similar pattern on his grid. Any number of objects can be used: pine cones, acorns, scissors, erasers, toy trucks. If a child can easily reproduce a pattern while yours is there for him to refer to, show him a pattern, then remove it and see if he can reconstruct it from memory. That encourages another level of development. Similar activities can be carried out using a flannel board and pieces of felt in different shapes and colors.

Artwork can be an important clue to the child's understanding of math concepts. When the child draws a person, is the order of the parts of the body correct? Does the head join the neck and the neck the body? At one stage of development many children show a head with two legs emerging beneath it. In addition, the proximity of body parts varies with the child's development—an immature drawing may contain all the body parts, but they may not be connected: a stomach floats next to a head and over some legs. You will find it extremely informative to have each child draw a person once a month and file them for reference. (See the chapter on record-keeping.)

One-to-One Correspondence and Graphing

The ability to match objects exactly with other objects—one-to-one correspondence—is a crucial skill in the child's mathematical development. It underlies his conception of the meaning of numbers and the performance of rote functions such as counting. In his daily life in the classroom there are many opportunities for developing this concept. Putting paintbrushes in the paint cans every morning, handing out scissors at a table to children who need them, putting napkins and cups out for a party, and setting up the snack table are some examples of how the child matches objects on a one-to-one basis.

Graphing is an excellent way of developing and reinforcing the idea of correspondence. Early experience with graphing should be as concrete and obvious as possible. Simple visual charts based on familiar stories are often effective. For example, after reading ''Three Little Pigs,'' a chart can be made with pictures of three pigs and a line connecting each pig with the kind of house he built. Actually using three-dimensional materials to suggest straw, sticks, and bricks will make the chart even more effective. Simple labels can be made for the pictures. Another chart can be made about "Goldilocks and the Three Bears." The children can match the right-size bear to the right-size bed, chair, and cereal bowl. If the figures are mounted on a bulletin board or a piece of fiberboard, and yarn is left hanging from the pictures of the bears, children can go over in their spare time and pin the other end of the yarn to the right implement.

Simple graphs about what children are wearing to school or how many children are present or absent or how many boys and girls are in the class can be represented visually with cutouts pasted in rows. A graph about pets owned by children in the class can be made by providing small cutouts of dogs, cats, turtles, fish, birds, and any other pets the children have. Each child pastes a picture of his pet in the appropriate row. In addition to contributing to the graph, children can dictate stories about their pets or, if they have no pet, about the pet they would like to have. Whenever a graph is made, it should be summarized with the children. For example, after the graph about pets is finished, display it to the class. Ask them how many children have dogs, how many have cats. They can also see at a glance which is the most common pet and which the least common. As they become more experienced in making and interpreting graphs, some of them can make their own by interviewing other children.

The following are some suggestions for topics for graphs. Many of them can be done almost independently by individuals or small groups of children. Of course, some children will need much more guidance than others.

1. **What's your favorite color?** An egg carton is filled with samples of different colored squares. Each child is asked to pick his favorite color from the egg carton and paste it on a sheet of graph paper in the row assigned to the particular color.

2. **What's your favorite holiday?** Paper cutouts of pumpkins, Christmas trees, birthday cakes, turkeys, and Easter bunnies are provided. Each child chooses the symbol that represents his favorite day and pastes it in the appropriate row on the paper.

3. What month is your birthday? Paper is ruled off into boxes three inches wide and one and a half inches high. Twelve different colors are used for cutting out paper rectangles three inches by one and a half inches. As each child comes to tell the month of his birthday, he writes his name on a piece of the appropriate color and it is pasted above the name of the right month. This graph should be done by an adult as many children will need help in writing their names if it is done early in the year, and many may not know the month of their birthday. This graph is a good one to have displayed in the room because it shows the range of ages at a glance. Often parents who are concerned about their child's progress can be reassured by seeing that children who may be doing "better" than their child are many months older.

4. Are you wearing ———? Many variations can be devised based on articles of clothing. Children can be asked whether they are wearing sneakers or regular shoes, whether they have shoelaces or buckles, whether they have long or short sleeves, socks, or trousers, whether they are wearing anything blue or red.

5. What's your favorite TV show? The candidates here can be suggested by the children. The interviewer may only want to ask about one show as opposed to another, or he may want to have five or six listed and ask the children to choose from this list.

6. Graphs may be made to show the results of experiments. After trying out a group of objects to see which float and which sink, a child can graph his results by coloring in the appropriate number of squares in each category. When he grows bean and pumpkin seeds, the plants can be measured every day and the results recorded on a graph.

7. Graphs may be used in making estimates. When the Halloween pumpkin is brought in, children can take turns guessing how much it weighs. Each child's name is written on the graph paper and the appropriate number of squares colored in to represent his guess. (When larger numbers are involved,

it is best to use smaller-grid paper rather than to have each square represent two or five since this can be confusing to the children.) After the pumpkin is weighed, the actual weight is recorded on the graph and comparisons can be made.

8. Graphs may be used to keep track of the weather. In addition to your weather chart, you can set up a graph with symbols for rainy days, cloudy days, sunny days, etc. Each day, as the weather is discussed, the appropriate symbol can be pasted in the correct row. At the end of the month, you can count how many rainy days there were, how many sunny, and record the totals.

9. When planning a meal to be eaten at school, the various choices children make can be recorded on a graph. This graph can be used as an aid in preparing the meal. Thus, if the graph shows that four children want tuna fish sandwiches and six want peanut butter and jelly, the children will know how many sandwiches of each kind to make.

10. How many letters in your name? Each child who is asked counts the letters in his name and records the result in either of two ways. He can color in the number of squares corresponding to the letters in his name, or he can actually write his name across the graph, using one space for each letter. (A more sophisticated graph would have a row for names of three letters, a row for names of four letters, and so forth, and each child would color in one square in the appropriate row. Since this and the following graphs represent two different numerations—in this case, the number of letters in names, and the number of children in each category—it should be saved until children are well acquainted with a variety of graphs.)

11. How many are in your family? Graph paper is set up with rows labeled 2, 3, 4, 5, 6, etc. Each child who is interviewed colors in a square in the row that tells how many are in his family.

12. How many buttons are you wearing? Rows are labeled from zero to ten. The child who is interviewed counts his buttons, then colors in the appropriate square.

Pegboards can also be used to develop skills in matching and one-to-one correspondence. This can be expanded to include the concept of more and less. After a child can easily match in his pegboard the number of pegs you have put in yours, see if he can make his row have one more peg than yours does. Can he give you one more, two more, five more when counting out pine cones, buttons, M & M's? The concept of what is more seems to be easier to grasp than the concept of less or fewer, and so it should be fully developed in a child before you begin asking him to show fewer pegs on his board than you have on yours and similar activities.

Many manipulative materials should be available in the math center for the children to experiment with and make their own discoveries about correspondence and matching. "Found" objects and retrieved junk make interesting objects for shoe box collections. Acorns, acorn caps, washers, beads, buttons, dried beans, popsicle sticks, rubber bands, matchsticks, birthday candles, bottle caps, spools, small plastic pill bottles are all materials which children enjoy handling, counting, sorting, and weighing.

Many games have been suggested in other chapters which involve keeping score. Tallying the score with toothpicks or buttons as counters (you get a toothpick every time you score a point) provides excellent practice in one-to-one matching and counting.

Counting and Concepts of Number

Counting is a complex skill that involves the ability to verbalize and to use symbols and an understanding of one-to-one correspondence. It is a mistake to assume that the ability to count by rote is all that is involved. Counting experiences help to develop many important concepts, including the meaning of numbers, one-to-one correspondence, more and less, and addition and subtraction.

In the classroom there are many opportunities for counting, such as keeping track of how many days there are until a holiday, noting which day of the month it is, or taking attendance. In taking attendance, let the children count with you and figure out how many are missing and who they are. As they record the weather, the children will be counting the number of rainy and sunny days. They may count how many fish are in the fish tank: how many gold and how many black. As they build a tower with blocks, they may count how many blocks they used to build it. (I found one way to get the block corner cleaned up quickly one year was to have the children count the blocks as they put them back. They were intrigued to know how many blocks they actually had out on the floor, and it passed the time as they put them away.) As they use pegboards they may count how many pegs it will take to fill up an entire board. At one time in our classroom a group of children spent their mornings for several days filling pegboards with pegs and stacking filled boards on top of one another to make a tower. They kept track of how many pegs they had used and were eager to have a tower which used a thousand pegs. Cooking experiences are full of opportunities for counting: How many tablespoons of sugar do we need? How many did we put in? How many cups of flour did we put in? How many cookies did we make? Are there enough for everyone to have two? When dramatizing a story, children may count: How many are needed to play billy goats? How many trolls? How many dwarfs? As they use the pegboard chart to go out in the hall (see Chapter 1) they need to count to see how many tags are already in place to determine if there is room for them at a particular activity.

In addition to the many experiences that grow out of daily life in the room, you can structure others to help the children clarify recognition of numerals and concepts of number. The children can help you make a reference chart showing the meaning of numbers from one to ten by stringing short lengths of string with different amounts of colored beads. They are arranged in numerical order and glued on heavy cardboard. Numerals are written opposite the strings. The board can be hung in the room at a convenient height so the children can go over and feel it if they need to check on a number. Also, the children can make a set of number cards. Have available pieces of shirt cardboard, glue, and an assortment of objects such as small pinecones, buttons, birthday candles, paper clips, small bars of soap, bottle caps, pieces of macaroni, etc. Write a numeral from one to ten on each of the cards with a felt-tip pen. Each child can then pick a card and glue the correct number of objects on it (five bars of soap, three bottle caps). The two activities just described can be done with small groups of children supervised by the teacher. In your initial inventory you will have seen which children have difficulty with number concepts: these are the children you should choose to help you make these aids.

You can help the children write number stories of the following kind: At home we have

1

house

2 cars

3 children

You write the words the child suggests and he can illustrate with pictures if he wishes.

At Halloween, pumpkin shapes with wide open mouths can be dittoed on orange poster paper, four pumpkins to a nine-by-twelve-inch page. They are then cut apart, and on the back of each one a numeral from one to nine is written. The children pick a pumpkin from the pile, and with crayon draw in the number of teeth in the pumpkin's mouth that is specified on the back of the paper.

Simple follow-the-dots drawings can be made, keyed to a holiday or unit: a pumpkin face, a tepee, a Christmas tree. You can make two different versions of the same drawing and put the numbers from one to ten on one drawing and higher numbers on the other. Then the children can choose the one they can do.

A long, thin piece of styrofoam can be lined off into nine segments and a numeral written in each square. It is put out with a box of colored toothpicks and the children poke toothpicks into each square according to the number written there.

Make a large number line in the hall for the children to walk on by cutting a strip of plain white shelf paper ten feet long and six inches wide. Make a heavy black line with magic marker one inch from the edge along the whole length. Mark the line at every six inches, and at each division write a numeral from one to twenty. Cover both sides of the shelf paper with transparent plastic adhesive paper. That will protect it from foot marks, and it can be wiped clean. The number line can then be taped to the floor and removed whenever necessary. Many activities can be done on the number line. Follow direction games can played (walk to 3, jump to 4, put your right hand on 5). A spinner can be made and two children can advance along the line according to the number they spin. A box of dominoes can be used: children can take a domino from the box and go to the number represented by the dots on the domino. On the playground asphalt, a number line can be drawn in colored chalk or painted with tempera. It can be drawn as a circle, spiral, or rectangle and the children can move along it as they wish when they are playing outdoors.

Using discarded floor tiles, you can make a set of numerals from one to ten that the children can lay out on the floor. They can put them in order, or place them in a pattern for a child to step on (1 on the left side, 2 on the right slightly ahead of the 1, 3 on the left slightly ahead of the 2, and so forth). Or the numerals can be placed in a straight line for hopping or jumping. Some sort of nonskid backing should be put on them if they are to be used that way, since otherwise they may slide, and a child could lose his balance.

At the beginning of each month, materials can be put out for the children to make their own calendars. At the beginning of the year this is quite a challenging activity, since many will have trouble forming numerals and sustaining a long job. But no pressure is put on them to do it unless they want to, and if they do, assistance is given as long as they need it. The forms are dittoed up in quantity and can be used each month. Several sample forms are filled in and left at the table so each of the four or five children who might be working at one time can have his own copy. When he is finished, the calendar is pasted on a large sheet of construction paper and the name of the month is written on it. If he wants to, the child can make a picture representative of the month with collage materials, crayon, chalk, or paint. After a few months, making the calendar becomes very easy for the children, and some will even make more than one.

month:

sun	mon	tues	wed	thurs	fri	sat

An understanding of cardinal numbers can be developed through conversations, stories (such as "The Five Chinese Brothers"), and poems. One such poem that can be used at Halloween is "Five Little Pumpkins":

Five little pumpkins sitting on the gate;
The first one said, "Oh my, it's getting late";
The second one said, "There are witches in the air";
The third one said, "Well, I don't care";
The fourth one said, "We sure are having fun!"

The fifth one said, "Let's run and run and run!"
Then oo-oo-oo-oo-oo went the wind and out went the lights.
And those five little pumpkins rolled out of sight.

A game that teaches cardinal numbers can be played either with the entire class or as you are waiting for all the children to arrive. First, choose five children to stand at the front of the room. Another child comes forward and is given a few props: a hat from the dress-up corner, a small truck, a book. Then he is directed to put the hat on the fourth child or to give the truck to the second child or to shake hands with the fifth child or to give the book to the second child.

Measurement

Measurement is an extremely good field for the development of many of the concepts already mentioned, as well as skills in estimating and comparing sizes of different objects. It is important to give children a great deal of experience using various materials as measures before using standard measures such as rulers, yardsticks, and scales. Length, weight, time, and liquid capacity can all be explored with kindergarten children.

To begin an exploration of length have available a variety of measuring units: scraps of yarn, string, ribbons of varying lengths, strips of cardboard, and sticks. Children can compare ribbons of various lengths by seeing which is longer and which is shorter, and they can arrange the ribbons in order from longest to shortest. Then children can find ribbons to match various lengths: the circumference of their waists or their wrists, their heights, the length of a chair, the circumference of a rubber ball. Classroom pets can be measured and their lengths compared. (In order to make this beginning measuring easier, it would be helpful if you precut some of the pieces of ribbon so that they correspond to certain measurements the children will be making.)

Body features can be measured with help from other children and adults. The teacher or another adult traces around the child's foot. He cuts it out, writes his name on it and compares it with other children's. Is his longer, fatter, smaller, wider? Wrists can be measured by wrapping them with yarn and cutting the yarn to size. To measure a child's height, have him lie down on the floor while another child lays building blocks along his side until they fit. A diagram of what blocks were used can be drawn. Children can use their hands to measure a table top.

At this point, if a child cannot compare lengths in different places—if he does not understand conservation of length (that two lengths may be the same size even when they are not right next to each other and so are not easily compared) he should not begin to use standard units of measure such as rulers or yardsticks. Instead, he should be encouraged to use every opportunity for comparing size and weight. Opportunities occur frequently in carpentry, block building, sewing, cooking, and art work. In all these activities he will be developing his math vocabulary as he uses words like bigger, heavier, smaller, thinner. In addition, children should be encouraged to estimate frequently, since estimating helps to strengthen and clarify important concepts. If the child needs a block to bridge a certain gap, he estimates which block will be the right size, and if his first guess is wrong he tries another until he finds one that will fit. A more difficult task is to estimate the difference between two objects that cannot be brought together for comparison. As the child's understanding advances, he can answer the question, Which is larger, the blackboard or the table? by comparing the two units with a ruler or yardstick and so confirm his guess.

Some children will be interested in how they might measure the size of the room. Various suggestions will be made as to how it could be done: line up all the chairs across the room, use a piece of string, have children lie down in a line across the room. After some or all of the suggested methods have been tried, you may pose the question whether it would be easier to measure the length of the room by laying out crayons in a long line, or by laying out long sticks. They may decide that sticks would be easier since you wouldn't need to use so many. At some point, some children will get the idea that you don't need many sticks, that one used over and over again will give the same result. But don't try to rush the development of this understanding by formulating it for them. It will come when they are ready for it.

The study of weight involves one of the most popular and useful activities in the math program—using a balance.[1] The simplest balances should not use numbers or standard weights, but merely two cups or trays balanced on a stick. They can be easily constructed (see the chapter on making things) or purchased commercially. In addition to these simple balances, other balances which use numbers and standard weights should be available for children's use. Many manipulative materials should be available for use with the balances: bottle caps, washers, sugar cubes, dried beans and peas, dry cereal, paper clips, crayons, erasers, pebbles, sand, and rice.

As you observe the children in their play with the balances, you can begin to offer some guidance to the ones who demonstrate some understanding of how to make things balance—that is, the ones who have some idea of conservation of weight. If you observe a child taking objects away from the heavier side of a balance to make the sides even, he is ready for directed activity. But many children will need to stay at a purely explorational level. They tend to take a "magical" approach to getting the scale to balance—they are thrilled when it happens, but have no strategy for making it happen again.

In the directed activity, begin by having children achieve a balance using different objects: acorns and sugar cubes, for example. You can have ready dittoed outline sketches of the balance, and after a child achieves a balance, he can record the results by drawing the objects on each side of the balance on the

[1]The activities suggested for the study of weight are adapted by permission of Schocken Books Inc. from Alvin Hertzberg and Edward F. Stone, SCHOOLS ARE FOR CHILDREN, New York, Schocken, 1971, pp. 77–83, © 1971 by Alvin Hertzberg and Edward F. Stone.

dittoed sketch. A simple sentence can be written: I balanced 3 acorns with 5 sugar cubes.

Then you can give him a specific problem: How many beans balance five paper clips? How many Cheerios balance three sugar cubes? When he learns to solve that kind of problem, you can begin to have him balance a group of objects with a single object: How many washers will it take to balance this wooden block? Here you are helping him to move toward the use of a standard weight. You can introduce the weight itself by asking him to weigh certain amounts of various substances. After he puts the one ounce weight in one pan, ask him to weigh one ounce of sugar cubes or beans, two ounces of rice, and so forth.

More advanced children can tackle such problems as: Weigh two ounces of sugar; when you put in two ounces more, how much do you have? Weigh eight ounces of rice, then take out three ounces; how much is left? The child can begin to use an actual scale—the type with a pan on one side for objects to be weighed, and on the other, a pan for standard weights, or whatever other models are available.

Another variation on the balance scale involves a flat stick with cup-hooks spaced along it at one-inch intervals. The child uses washers to make it balance. A good commercial version of this device, called E.S.A. Equaliser Balance, is available from Educational Supply Assoc., Ltd., Schools Materials Division, Pinnacles, P.O. Box 22, Harlow, Essex CM19 5AY, England. It demonstrates that a weight placed at the number 2 on the scale and a weight placed at the number 4 will be balanced by a weight placed on the other side of the fulcrum at 6. Many important discoveries can be made with this scale by the children. It is helpful to have them make sketches occasionally of what they see after they have made a balance. That encourages them to observe how the balance works.

Liquid measurement is used extensively in cooking, and vocabulary can be developed here: cup, pint, quart. When you are getting ready to fill the aquarium, ask the children to guess how many gallons or quarts it will take to fill it. Their guesses can be recorded on a graph and then compared with the actual result. The same thing can be done when filling the water table. Water table equipment should include measuring spoons, measuring cups, and pint-, quart-, and gallon-sized containers. Water table play can be varied at times by adding soapsuds or food coloring to the water.

Measurement of time should be cued to the child's experience. Begin with discussions of school time, lunch time, days of the week, seasons, and perhaps phases of the moon. A weather chart can be kept. A calendar should be on display and discussed each day during the opening. You might have both a calendar showing a whole month at a time and one which shows only a day at a time. The children can make their own calendars each month (see page 68).

Kindergarten children can learn to tell time by the hour and many can learn the half hour as well. Some kindergarten children and many first graders will learn the whole system of telling time. Using charts, the times for various all-class activities can be displayed: art class, 9:30; playground, 10:30; dismissal, 12:00. Children enjoy making large clocks that can be worn around their waists or made into huge pocket watches. Each child is given a circle of heavy paper six inches in diameter. It is easier for him to keep his numbers spaced evenly if dots are placed at appropriate intervals around the edge. After he writes in the numerals, he cuts out a big and little hand and fastens them to the center of the circle with a brass fastener. The watch is stapled to two long pieces of paper to make a "wristwatch" suitable for wearing around his waist, or he can make a paper chain four or five links long (out of six inch strips) if he prefers a "pocket watch."

Space Relationships and Geometric Shapes

Another important aspect of the early math program is to develop an awareness of shapes, lines, and angles in every day objects. At the beginning of the year, basic shapes can be introduced and reviewed. Many children will already have some familiarity with the names of the shapes. Circles can be traced and turned into pumpkin faces at Halloween. If you make pancakes at school, ask the children if they eat any other foods shaped like a circle. Make a circle picture-chart: Children draw pictures of things that are round, or they cut out magazine pictures, and they paste the pictures on a large sheet of paper. Underneath each object its name is printed. For an independent activity, provide children with cutout circles of different sizes and colors so that the children may arrange them on colored paper in pleasing designs.

Another project that uses circles in an interesting way requires the preparation of many four-by-four-inch squares of colored paper with a circle traced on each one. (A large frozen orange juice can makes a good guide.) Each child takes six squares and carefully cuts out the circles. Five circles are folded in half, then slit in the middle almost to the edge. The sixth circle is left unfolded and uncut. The folded circles are mounted on the flat circle around its edge. When the edges are adjusted, a star is formed.

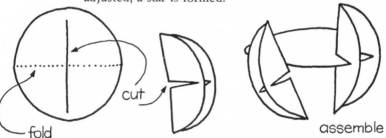

Metal or cardboard forms can be used by the children in tracing circles and other geometric shapes. Designs can be made by combining tracings of circles of different sizes. The use of a template provides excellent practice in using fine motor skills.

Sketch a roadway on the floor using chalk or two pieces of masking tape. Pose the following problem to the children: Can you travel down this road making a circle? Encourage them to solve the problem in as many ways as possible. I have seen children respond by forming a circle with their fingers or hands or arms as they traveled, by twirling their bodies around along the length of the roadway and by turning somersaults.

Similar activities can be devised for the square, rectangle, and triangle. Your point is not just to have the children know the names of the shapes, but to begin to develop an awareness of squareness, roundness, and the rest, and to begin to learn how shapes are used in many ways around them.

Geoboards are interesting and useful tools for developing concepts of space and shape. Direction for making them are contained in the chapter on making things. They are also available from commercial sources. The first phase in working with geoboards, as with all math equipment, is unstructured exploration. After the child has had a good deal of experience with the equipment, he will then enjoy being posed certain problems. You might begin by asking him to make all the shapes he can with the rubber bands on the board and then naming the shapes. He can start with a shape, pull out one side, and talk about what happens, for example, to the length of the sides, to the corners, to the direction the sides take, and so forth. Show the child a parallelogram. Ask him if he can make it into a rectangle? Can he do it with only one movement? Can he turn it into a square? Can he turn a triangle into a square? Have the child make a square whose sides are three squares long. Ask him how many squares are contained in the large square.

A kinesthetic approach to shapes is featured in a game in which the child stands behind a screen or behind a cardboard box with a hole cut in it for his hands to reach through. He is given a shape to feel: then he tries to point to the same shape on a large chart.

A game called "Robot" is extremely popular with children and helps to develop their awareness of direction and ways of moving through space. A child is chosen to be the robot. He is blindfolded, and told he can only move upon the command of one other child designated to be the director. An object is put in plain sight somewhere in the room, and the director tries to guide the robot to the object by giving him the proper directions: take three steps forward, turn to your left, lift your right hand, and so forth. This game is quite challenging for young children because it calls for breaking movements down into component parts and the child who is giving the directions must think carefully about what he is saying. It would be helpful to have an adult be the robot the first time, to show how the robot must do exactly what the director says (children may forget to tell him to stop, may say right when they mean left, and so forth) and must not interpret what the director meant to say.

Books for Teachers

- Baretta-Lorton, Mary, WORKJOBS II: NUMBER ACTIVITIES FOR EARLY CHILDHOOD, Reading, Mass., Addison-Wesley, 1979.

- Biggs, Edith and Maclean, James R., FREEDOM TO LEARN, An Active Learning Approach to Mathematics, Reading, Mass., Addison-Wesley, 1969.

- Brown, Sam E., ONE, TWO, BUCKLE MY SHOE: MATH ACTIVITIES FOR YOUNG CHILDREN, Mt. Rainier, Md., Gryphon House, 1982.

- Holt, Michael, and Dienes, Zoltan, LET'S PLAY MATH, New York, Walker and Company, 1973.

- Zaslavsky, Claudia, PREPARING YOUNG CHILDREN FOR MATH: A BOOK OF GAMES, New York, Schocken, 1979.

Books for Children

- Anno, Mitsumatsa, ANNO'S COUNTING BOOK, New York, Philomel, 1982.

- Bangs, Molly, TEN, NINE, EIGHT, New York, Greenwillow, 1983.

- Barr, Catherine, SEVEN CHICKS MISSING, New York, Henry Z. Walck, 1962.

- Bishop, Claire H., FIVE CHINESE BROTHERS, New York, Coward, McCann & Geoghegan, 1938 and Eau Claire, Wisc., E. M. Hale, 1938.

- Crews, Donald, TEN BLACK DOTS, New York, Scribner, 1968.

- Eichenberg, Fritz, DANCING IN THE MOON: COUNTING RHYMES, New York, Harcourt Brace Jovanovich, 1956.

- Elkin, Benjamin, SIX FOOLISH FISHERMAN, Chicago, Childrens Press, 1957.

- Emberley, Barbara (adapted by), ONE WIDE RIVER TO CROSS, Englewood Cliffs, N.J., Prentice-Hall, 1966.

- Feelings, Muriel, MOJA MEANS ONE: SWAHILI COUNTING BOOK, New York, Dial, 1971.

- Francoise, JEANNE-MARIE COUNTS HER SHEEP, New York, Scribner, 1957.

- Friskey, Margaret, CHICKEN LITTLE, COUNT-TO-TEN, Chicago, Childrens Press, 1946.

- Gag, Wanda, MILLIONS OF CATS, New York, Coward, McCann & Geoghegan, 1938.

- Hoberman, Mary Ann and Hoberman, Norman, ALL MY SHOES COME IN TWOS, Boston, Little, Brown, 1957.

- Ipcar, Dahlov, BROWN COW FARM: A COUNTING BOOK, New York, Doubleday, 1959.
  TEN BIG FARMS, New York, Knopf, 1958.

- Kredenser, Gail, ONE DANCING DRUM, New York, S. G. Phillips, 1971.

- Langstaff, John and Rojankovsky, Feodor, OVER IN THE MEADOW, New York, Harcourt Brace Jovanovich, 1967.

- Lionni, Leo, INCH BY INCH, Stamford, Conn., Astor-Honor, 1962.

- McLeod, Emilie W., ONE SNAIL AND ME, Boston, Little, Brown, 1961.

- Maestro, Giulio, ONE MORE AND ONE LESS, New York, Crown, 1974.

- Meeks, Esther K., ONE IS THE ENGINE, Chicago, Follett, 1972.

- Myller, Rolf, HOW BIG IS A FOOT?, New York, Atheneum, 1962.

- Schlein, Miriam, HEAVY IS A HIPPOPOTAMUS, Reading, Mass., Addison-Wesley (Young Scott Books), 1954.

- Sendak, Maurice, CHICKEN SOUP WITH RICE: A BOOK OF MONTHS, New York, Harper & Row, 1952 and Scholastic Book Services (Star-Line), 1970.

- Seuss, Dr., THE FIVE HUNDRED HATS OF BARTHOLOMEW CUBBINS, Eau Claire, Wisc., E. M. Hale, 1938.

4

record-keeping and planning

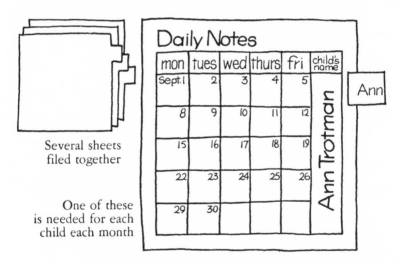

Several sheets filed together

One of these is needed for each child each month

Daily Notes

mon	tues	wed	thurs	fri	child's name
Sept. 1	2	3	4	5	
8	9	10	11	12	
15	16	17	18	19	Ann Trotman
22	23	24	25	26	
29	30				

Ann

Record-Keeping

One of the most important aspects of running a successful open classroom is the keeping of detailed records on each child in order to have a picture of what he does, what he is learning, and how you need to help him. Whenever you are working with a child you will want to keep notes on what you are doing, and in addition you will want to record the observations you make of the children while they are on their own.

I found the record-keeping system described in this chapter to work very well, both when I was in the room by myself and when I had helpers. When there were student teachers or aides in the room, I asked them to be responsible for taking notes and entering them on the master sheet for whatever activities they were responsible for.

The notes were kept on an individual sheet for each student for each month. All sheets for one month were fastened together with paper fasteners and indexed by first name. When the month was over, the forms were taken apart and the sheets were filed in each child's folder.

One index was made for each class. But because it was cumbersome to go flipping through so many pages each time I wanted to jot down an entry while working with a child, I also used a class list of each child's name with a space by each for comments. It was more convenient to use the list during the day, and at the end of the day it took only a few minutes to transfer the day's notes to each child's master sheet. Whenever I had a student teacher or an aide or a high school student working on an activity with a child, I gave them a class list and asked them to make notes of children's reactions as they worked with them. Of course the quality of the observations varied. But the experience of recording was as valuable to the people doing it as it was to me. It forced them to think about what was going on and to put into words their observations of the children. This resulted in more specific and pertinent observations. And whenever possible we also discussed the results they had seen so that they got more ideas of what to look for and what things were important to notice.

Here are excerpts from comments recorded on one child's sheets during a period of several months:

Water-painting on the blackboard: difficulty following directions, consistently reversed until he tried it in the salt box, then was able to do it.

Gingerbread man story: made very tiny drawings, wanted to do whole story, asked for help with sequence; had difficulty hearing unless he looked at me.

Worked hard on calendar; sat all by himself.

Good concept of rhyme—can supply rhyming words easily, makes up own rhymes.

Sink or float experiment: involved, made predictions—if one paper clip sank, the rest will sink; generalized about what would happen.

Very short attention span for small group activities; prefers working by himself.

Identifies most initial consonant-sounds readily; loves to play games using sounds.

Needs much help with small muscle coordination: some trouble using scissors, holding pencil, etc.

And from another:

Forgetful, but willing and cheerful; tried to write her name, did first three letters; leaves crayon or finished work behind.

Recognized her name written, but doesn't know names of letters except *f*. Very eager to try tracing her name, used firm confident strokes, elated with results and wanted to do it again.

Difficulty recognizing numerals 2 through 9.

Number Lotto: some difficulty recognizing numbers, but got better as game progressed; loved playing.

Halloween book: eager to make one but could not copy *W* without help; in copying *CAT* started with *T* and worked to the left; has trouble beginning at left; doesn't copy letters in order.

Told a story—using completely unrelated sentences.

Worked on letter recognition: learned *A* very easily, very interested, wanted to stay.

During the course of the year, many similar comments and observations were recorded about each child. Of course if you have people helping you in your room, you will have more notes about each child than if you are alone, but even if you are the only person who is taking the notes, you will be surprised at what a good picture of the child you will have as the months go by. When you are writing out a report card or talking with a parent you will have very specific comments to make which will be very useful in getting your points across.

Along with the monthly sheets, we put into the child's folder a self-portrait each month. At the beginning of each month we asked each child to draw a picture of himself and write his name on it. These were dated and put into his folder. During the course of the year there were some amazing changes in the way children drew themselves. When we had conferences with the psychologist about certain children, these drawings were very revealing. Immature children in particular often made great growth in their perception of themselves and the way they drew their pictures.

Other files were kept according to subject-area. When there were several children who did not recognize their name, their names were put on a folder with that information on the front. Children who knew all the initial consonants and were ready for more advanced work were listed on another folder. Children who needed help in counting and in recognition of numbers were listed on yet another folder, and so forth. The folders each contained suggestions for activities to be done with these children on the subjects in question. When I had a student teacher or volunteer (not a parent) who was looking for something to do, she could take a folder and do some work with children who needed help in one or another area. Working on a particular skill gave the student teachers a chance to follow through with a variety of activities and helped them evaluate the progress the children were making. In many cases the student teachers devised extremely useful techniques and games for dealing with some of these skills.

Planning

Careful planning of activities for an informal classroom is essential to keep the environment stimulating and varied. When you are setting up a new unit of study, it should be planned several weeks ahead of the time you will actually be using it in the classroom. That will allow you plenty of time to order films, books, and other materials from school and local libraries. It will give you time to gather background material and to plan various ways of involving children in activities related to the unit. If any special cooking or other projects will be a part of the unit, you can arrange for volunteers to be on hand to help. Once you have used a unit with the children, and have made any additions and changes dictated by your experience of it in the classroom, your plans can be filed away along with any samples of student work, pictures, charts, and other materials that will be helpful for you when you use the unit again. The next time you use it, much less work will be involved in preparing it, although you will still want to allow time to procure materials that must be ordered in advance.

To plan the day-to-day activities that will be going on in the room independent of the study unit you can usually work about a week or so ahead of time. Of course, certain activities will continue throughout the year and will not have to be planned for each week. They include the block corner, the housekeeping area, the easels, the library corner, the snack, and the animals. Supplies may need to be replenished from time to time, and you will want to vary the books and records frequently in the library corner, but basically these activities are self-sustaining. You will need to plan for various independent activities and activities done with adult help that are not part of the ongoing routine of the class. In deciding which art or cooking projects you want to provide for the children for the coming week, you will be thinking about how they might fit into the current study unit, whether a volunteer helper will be needed to assist the children, and whether additional supplies will need to be bought or contributed by the children. Some projects should be carried on for more than one day in order to give everyone a chance to participate as often as they wish, while others can be discontinued after one day. Math and science activities may require that special materials be assembled, and in some cases you will want to prepare summary sheets where the children can record their findings—blank graph paper, calendar blanks, pattern cards for use with pegboards and beads, sketches of a balance apparatus on which they can draw the results of their experiments, and so forth. Here, also, it is important to have included work for volunteers in your plans, if volunteers are coming in, since you will definitely want to avoid the awkwardness and also the waste of not having anything for a volunteer to do. All of this planning, done a week or more ahead of time, saves you from frantic rushing to get a mother in two days before you are ready to begin a project, or even worse, preparing to start a project one day and realizing that an essential ingredient is missing.

Once you have set up the various activities that will be going on in the room during the activity period, the important remaining planning is for the work you will be doing with individual children. It is much more difficult to plan this ahead of time because you will never know what different children may accomplish in one day, or what work they will be interested in doing on another day. Instead it should be done at the end of each day, while you are transferring your notes onto the master record sheet. Then you will be reviewing what many children have done during the day. Of course you will not have a comment for each child unless your class is small or unless you have a lot of help. But over the course of a week, you should be in touch with what each child has done. At this time you can think about what you might do with the child the next day. Johnny wrote a story about spacemen to go with his picture; tomorrow I'll show him the map of the moon. Debbie has been asking how to spell words; tomorrow we will write a letter. Jane and Ellen have been working on initial consonants; tomorrow they can make a book and spell the words.

This does not mean that you will plan to spend a few minutes with each child every day. You may not work with a child at all for three or four days, then spend a half hour with him the next day. All the time that the child is busy in the room, he is growing and learning, particularly if you are providing an interesting environment with many opportunities for new experiences. Even if you could provide it, he does not need, and is better off without, your undivided attention every minute of the day. However, it is easy in a large class to find that you have seen some children frequently and others hardly at all during a given period. In your daily referral to your record sheets, as you record activities and comments, you will note which children you are seeing and how often. If you find that you have unintentionally neglected a chid, you might plan some specific things to do with him in the next few days.

Of course, there are times when you may deliberately refrain from working with a child for a reason. He may be under parental pressure to become involved in academic subjects and hence have developed a distaste for anything remotely connected with them. He will need time to become interested in certain activities that other children found fascinating to begin with. Or you may have a child who is socially immature and who needs a great deal of time to develop his relationships with other children. All of these judgments on your part require the same sensitivity and understanding of your students' needs that are a prerequisite of a good teacher in any situation.

To help you in the end-of-the-day planning, it is a good idea to have various materials already assembled in several content areas, so that you do not have to make them up each day. For example, in working with initial consonants, it is useful to have magazine pictures of things that begin with different letters. A collection of these pictures can be added to every time you finish reading a magazine. Also, you may want to cut out pages from workbooks, cover them with clear plastic, and make them available as review material. When you are working with number concepts, it will be useful to have already prepared various materials such as kinesthetic number cards, flash cards with numerals and the number of objects represented, objects to count, and follow-the-dot papers.

If you have student teachers and/or an aide working with you, the planning is best done cooperatively. Of course, you as the teacher are responsible for what goes on in the room, but others who will be working there with you should be included in the planning, so that the goals you are working toward and the techniques to be used will be familiar to them as well. It is especially important that student teachers be given an increasing amount of responsibility in planning for the class, because planning is one of the most crucial skills they will need as they set up their own classrooms. Also, student teachers and aides may in planning sessions suggest ideas drawn from their own interests and strengths and so add to the classroom.

5

the unit approach

Using the unit approach in an open classroom allows you to center many of your activities and suggestions for the children on a particular theme or subject. It adds interest for the children and increases the material they are exposed to. It also provides many opportunities for you as a teacher to help the children acquire important skills in an interesing setting. The basic setup of the room is the same, and many ongoing activities, such as the block corner, easels, water table and snack, continue as usual, but the focus in other areas will be upon the particular unit being studied. The art projects, cooking, music, games, math, reading readiness, and language development can all be developed around a central topic.

Many units which you already use in your classroom can be adapted to a more informal classroom setup. You will need to rearrange activities that formerly were done by the whole class under your supervision so that they can be done by children in small groups or by themselves, either with supervision or alone. In addition, units may be suggested by the children in the class, as an outgrowth of something brought in to show, or perhaps prompted by a unit already in progress.

This chapter offers suggestions for two units, one on American Indians and one on health and nutrition entitled "You and Your Body." Each can serve as the basis for several weeks of activity in the classroom. With the unit approach, you will see how a particular theme can be used to great advantage in an informal setup. The children are always busy making things, learning to use their bodies in new ways, and acquiring new skills in a highly motivating environment. You will find that the interest and excitement generated by the children is contagious, and you may discover new fascination in topics you thought had been exhausted long ago.

Indians

Young children are almost invariably fascinated by Indians. Unfortunately, their impressions are too often formed by blood-and-thunder cowboy movies or television shows that emphasize violence and negative aspects of Indian culture. A unit about Indians in the kindergarten begins by capitalizing on the children's natural interest in a colorful aspect of American culture but the unit moves on to help break down stereotypes by conveying information on a broad range of aspects of Indian life, such as arts and crafts, language, music and dancing, cooking, and games. Other concepts that can be developed as the unit progresses include the Indians as the first Americans and the position of Indians today. (Some live on reservations while others have become active in the larger society in government, business, art, and other fields. Maria Tallchief, the famous ballerina, is one example; the Mohawks, whose agility at great heights makes them excellent construction workers on tall buildings and bridges, are another.) Contributions made by Indian culture to modern life can also be brought out. Two examples that suggest themselves immediately are foods used first by North American Indians and still used today, and common words and place names which came from Indian languages (succotash, Massachusetts, etc.)

A good introduction to the unit is to talk with the children about Indians, asking them to tell you what they know. This will give you a picture of what concepts they have about Indians and it allows them to express some of the things they might want to learn about in the upcoming weeks. It is important to have as many pictures around the room as possible to help supply the children with information. Copy some typical Indian designs on large pieces of heavy paper and have them available for the children to use when they are making Indian objects which they want to decorate.

Indian Language

Indians of many different tribes relied on picture-writing to communicate with other tribes when they did not share a common language. Stories written with picture-symbols accompanying the words provide an interesting introduction to picture-language. *Little Elk Hunts Buffalo* and *Painted Pony Runs Away*[1] are good examples of such stories. After the children have heard one of the stories and have had a chance to look at the book several times, they may be interested in learning a few pictographs. Working with perhaps four children at a time, you can help the children copy various symbols. This activity gives practice in following step-by-step directions, in eye-hand coordination, and in copying a design, all important pre-reading and pre-writing skills. The children can choose the designs they wish to include in a book. After they have made as many designs as they want (two may be more than enough for children whose coordination is poor, while others will enjoy making four or five), the pictures can be stapled together to form the book, which can be given a title.

Later, children can be encouraged to develop their own picture-symbols for words that are important to them. Working with an adult, a small group of children can compose a short story and translate it into pictures to be read to the whole class.

Now is a good time to start a chart of Indian words that the children encounter as they hear stories and learn about Indians. This chart can be displayed where everyone can see it, and it can be added to as necessary. Words that might be a part of such a chart include: **TEPEE, WIGWAM, TOTEM POLE, TOM-TOM, PAPOOSE, CANOE.**

Making picture books with one-word labels (see page 38) is a good way for children to become familiar with many of the Indian words and to be able to "read" them. Simple line drawings of Indian objects are drawn on six-by-nine-inch sheets of oaktag. The names of the objects are printed underneath and each card is covered with clear adhesive paper. (This allows children

[1] Jessie Brewer McGraw, Camden N.J., Thomas Nelson and Sons.

Here are some picture-symbols, and the steps for children to follow in making them.

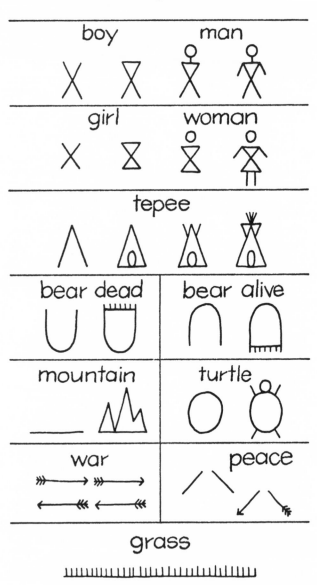

to trace over the letters with their crayon if they need help in forming the letters, and the pictures can be cleaned easily by rubbing with a soft cloth.) The cards are left on a table for the children to use as guides in preparing their own. After they have finished, the pages are fastened together into a book.

An interesting part of an exploration of Indian language can be an excursion into sign language. An excellent book for this purpose is *Indian Sign Language* by Robert Hofsinde (Gray-Wolf).[2] All children love secret messages and special languages, and there are simple signs in Hofsinde's that kindergarten children can easily learn. In one section, he gives the Indian names for the months, with appropriate hand signals. These names provide a good springboard for discussion: why did the Indians name the months as they did? What names are still meaningful today? They also provide a takeoff point for pictures and dramatic play that illustrate what might take place during each month in an Indian village.

These are the names:

January	Snow Moon
February	Hunger Moon
March	Crow Moon
April	Green Grass Moon
May	Planting Moon
June	Rose Moon
July	Thunder Moon
August	Green Corn Moon
September	Hunting Moon
October	Falling Leaf Moon
November	Mad Moon
December	Long Night Moon

If you have access to a woodland area, (perhaps your playground would suffice) you can show the children some Indian trail markings. It would be fun to set up a simple trail in advance and have the children follow the signs. They would first need to learn the signs, and they could practice setting them up in the room until they were sure of them.

[2]Robert Hofsinde, INDIAN SIGN LANGUAGE, New York, Morrow, 1956.

These signs would be useful
in setting up a trail.

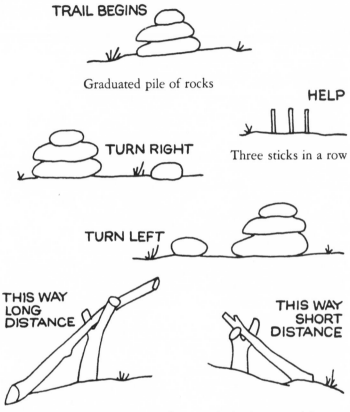

TRAIL BEGINS

Graduated pile of rocks

HELP

Three sticks in a row

TURN RIGHT

TURN LEFT

**THIS WAY
LONG
DISTANCE**

**THIS WAY
SHORT
DISTANCE**

In addition, the children might be interested in
learning these two signs:

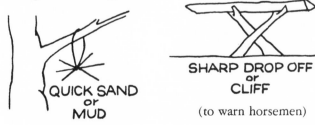

**QUICK SAND
or
MUD**

Three sticks in a bunch
hanging from a tree

**SHARP DROP OFF
or
CLIFF**

(to warn horsemen)

Indian Games

There are several Indian games that can be adapted for young children to play. Besides providing good activities for children to undertake together without supervision, the games help to develop muscle coordination. In keeping score, concepts of counting and number are developed. Making the apparatus for the games is also a good independent activity for the children.

Stick Game

You need several pieces of cardboard one and a half inches wide by eight inches long to form the sticks. One side should be decorated with Indian designs made with crayon or felt-tip pen. Each child can make his own stick. To play, children take turns tossing their sticks in the air. If the painted side lands facing up, the child gets a point. Toothpicks or buttons can be provided for keeping score. When a child gets a point, he takes a button and places it in his paper cup. After the game is over, children count their markers and the winner is established. (Deciding who is the winner may not be so simple as it seems. After one such game had been completed in our classroom, the following question was asked: "We don't know who won. She has twenty-three and I have thirty-four. Who has the most?")

Bean Toss

This game[3] requires dried lima beans marked on one side with a small dot. Ten or fifteen beans are placed in a shallow dish and flipped gently onto the table. The score is obtained by counting the number of beans with dots showing. Again, the score can be kept with toothpicks or other markers.

Hidden Ball Game

You need four small cans such as frozen juice cans decorated with Indian signs. One person hides a small pebble under one of the cans and the other player tries to guess which one it is hidden under.

[3]Adaptation of Bowl Game from INDIAN GAMES AND CRAFTS by Robert Hofsinde, New York, Morrow, 1957, pp. 1–19, © 1957 by Robert Hofsinde, and adapted by permission of William Morrow & Co., Inc.

Kick Stick

This is a good outdoor game.[4] You need two sticks, each about a foot long and one inch thick. Indian designs can be painted on the sticks. The players try to kick the sticks around a circle. The first to get his stick back to the starting place is the winner.

Turtle Toss and Ring Toss

These two games can be made for children to play by themselves.[5] For the turtle toss, a turtle shape is cut out of a six-inch square of oaktag. The shape is colored and holes are punched as shown in the drawing. The turtle is fastened to a dowel or to some other thin stick by a string about eight inches long. Holding on to the stick and tossing the turtle, the child tries to catch one of the holes on the stick.

For Ring Toss, a buffalo head with horns is cut out of heavy paper and fastened to a stick. Two strings are attached to the center of the head. Each string has a ring fastened at the other end. The child tries to catch one or both rings on the buffalo horns.

[4]Adapted from Zuni Kick Stick, INDIAN GAMES AND CRAFTS, pp. 20–25, by permission of William Morrow & Co., Inc.

[5]Adapted from Toss and Catch, INDIAN GAMES AND CRAFTS, pp. 77–85, by permission of William Morrow & Co., Inc.

Indian Homes

The place where a tribe lived influenced the type of housing it used. Nomadic tribes such as the Apaches made tepees out of animal hide and disassembled them when they moved on to a new hunting ground. Cliff dwellers of the southwest used the stone outcroppings as the basis for their many-tiered pueblos. Eastern woodlands tribes built long houses of logs or wigwams of saplings and bark. Each type can be reproduced in miniature by young children.

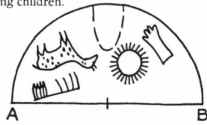

To make a tepee, provide a semicircular pattern that is placed on brown paper, traced, and cut out. Decorations are made along the curved edge. Side A in the drawing is brought over to Side B to form the tepee shape. Then the two ends are stapled together. A door can be cut in the bottom and twigs inserted in the hole at the top to imitate the poles used to support the tepee.

A large tepee, which children can get in and out of, can be made for the classroom. Three stout poles or branches of approximately equal height are lashed together at the top to form a tripod. After they have been set in place, old sheets which have been decorated with felt-tip pen are hung over the poles.

Pueblo houses can be made by painting shoe boxes brown or by smearing them with mud and letting it dry. Then they can be arranged to create several layers of dwellings with small ladders leading from one story to another. Another possibility is to build them with sugar cubes, one layer at a time. This is a challenging project, which is perhaps best done by a group of children working together with an adult.

The wigwam, used by tribes from the Great Lakes and farther east, was based on a frame of bent saplings, which was then covered with grass or bark. With kindergarten children, wigwams are duplicated most easily with play dough; grass, twigs and bark are pressed into the surface before it hardens. Or they can be formed with papier-mâché over an oblong ball of newspaper.

A wigwam for children to play in can be made from the kind of large cardboard box that refrigerators and other large appliances are delivered in. Doors can be cut in each end and the box can be painted and then decorated with grass and twigs.

The longhouses of the woodlands tribes can be built from Lincoln logs. A two-dimensional representation can be made by gluing straight pretzel sticks to a sheet of cardboard to fill in the outline.[6]

Indian Costumes and Decorations— Indian Beads

Any of the play dough recipes (found in Chapter 8) can be used for forming Indian beads. The children can measure the ingredients and help to make the play dough. You can color several different batches with food coloring as you mix the dough, or the children can paint the finished beads after they dry. Beads are formed by rolling a ball the size of a cherry tomato and piercing it carefully with a lollypop stick to make a hole. The beads are left to dry for several days. Egg cartons make good individual storage containers for each child to keep his beads in.

Nylon thread or fishing line makes good string for threading the beads, since it is stiff and easy to handle and does not break easily. Colorful buttons, plastic straws cut into one and two inch lengths, and pieces of macaroni can be provided to string with the clay beads. The macaroni can be colored ahead of time by mixing thin tempera paint, pouring it into a shallow tray, and rolling the macaroni around in it for several seconds. If you let the macaroni stay in the paint too long it will start to soften. The painted macaroni is then spread on newspaper to dry.

If you have colored wooden beads in the room, this is a good time to work with sequence and patterns. Start a pattern of beads on a string and see if a child can complete it. First patterns should be simple, with only one variable. As the child's skill increases, increase the number of variables. Provide a series of pattern cards and put them on the table where the beads and strings are kept.

[6]An excellent source for the teacher is INDIANS AT HOME by Robert Hofsinde, New York, Morrow, 1964.

Indian Brave's Headband

A strip of oaktag is cut long enough to encircle the child's head. Before it is stapled to fit, he decorates it as he sees fit. One method gives more practice in patterning. Provide a number of small geometric shapes in different colors. Gummed paper is good for this because it eliminates the need for pasting. The child makes up his own pattern and repeats it around the headband. Or, he can choose from among several sample patterns and repeat it around the headband.

Making feathers to go on the headband can provide more math experience. Provide rectangles cut out of colored paper, three inches wide and seven or more inches long. Arrange them in piles on a table according to color. Then the child picks up a card with numbers written in different colors and uses the card as a guide when choosing his feathers. He must read the number, recognize the color it is printed in and count the right numbers of feathers in each color. By trimming the corners off the top of the rectangle, feathers are quickly made. Cutting fringe around the edges is especially good in exercising the fine muscles in a child's hand. The feathers are then stapled to the headband and the headband stapled to fit the child's head. A small hand staple should be made available for the children's use.

Chief's War Bonnet

For each bonnet, two sheets of brown paper, one twenty-four by six inches, and the other twelve by six inches, are needed. Fold each sheet of paper in half lengthwise, so that you have sheets twenty-four by three inches and twelve by three inches. Bend the longer sheet around and fit the shorter piece between the ends of the longer one. Staple it to fit the child's

head. Now feathers are cut, as for the brave's headband, and they are inserted
all around the
headpiece and
down the back.

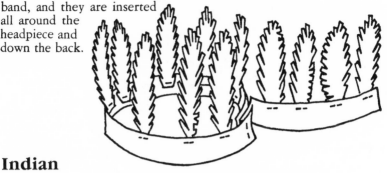

Indian
Vests

These can be made out of large grocery bags
or old pillow cases. For the grocery bag vest:

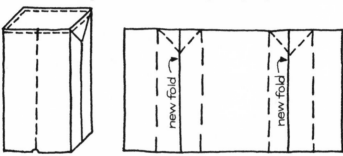

1. Cut up the center of the bag and cut out the bottom.
2. Refold it as indicated.

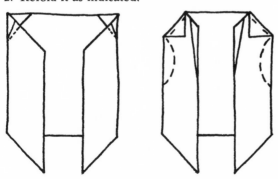

3. Make a V-shaped pleat at the top corners of the bag
(the line of the bag will guide you). Staple to form the
shoulder. 4. Mark cutting lines for a V-neck and arm

holes. The child cuts the neck and arm holes, fringes the bottom, then decorates as desired.

To make a vest out of a pillowcase cut out the arm holes and neck hole, but do not slit front all the way to the bottom. Felt-tip pens are better than crayons for decorating cloth.

Armbands and Wristlets

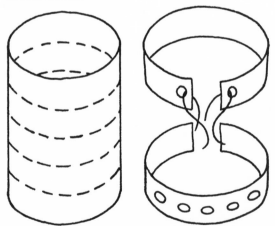

You will need several empty oatmeal or other round cardboard boxes. Cut one-and-a-half-inch sections from the box. The child trims the piece to fit his wrist, punches a hole in each end, and pushes a piece of yarn through each hole for ties. For decorations, holes can be punched all along the edge and threaded with colorful yarn (manipulating a hole punch is another good exercise for small hands). Or layers of crepe paper can be fringed and glued to the strip.

Wampum Strips

Shell macaroni makes a good substitute for wampum. It can be dyed with tempera paint (see page 165). A strip of heavy oaktag or cardboard ten inches long and two inches wide provides the base for the strip. At the simplest level, the children are given cards with numbers printed in different colors. They read the numbers on the card and glue the wampum on their strip according to the card: five yellows and three greens, or two reds and three blues. For more advanced children, you can assign a numerical value to each color (as Indians did in using real wampum). For example, red might equal three, blue two, and green one. Then give the child a number and ask him to represent it on his wampum strip using whatever combination of colors he can. It may seem a difficult task, but you can be sure that in many classes there will be at least a few children who are ready for this type of challenge, and they should be getting it.

Indian Makeup

A collection of odds and ends of women's makeup—rouge, eyeshadow, and lipstick—may be used for face painting. Be sure you have an adequate supply of cold cream for removing the paint, though. A paste of cocoa and water can be mixed and smeared on the face, and other designs added over it. Theatrical greasepaint can also be used.

Indian Music and Dancing—Drums

To make a large drum for the classroom, find a discarded wooden nail keg. Remove the bottom and top and paint the keg. For the drum heads, old inner tubes make a good substitute for leather. Cut two circles whose diameters are four inches larger than the top of the drum. Punch holes all around the outer edge two inches apart and one inch from the edge. Stretch the circle over the top of the keg and wind twine around it to hold it in place temporarily. Place the other circle around the bottom of the keg and secure it with twine also. Then lace a heavy thong or twine back and forth between the top and bottom circles. Pull the twine tight to produce the tone, but be careful of tearing the rubber. This drum or a similar large drum is used to accompany the Indian dances described later.[7]

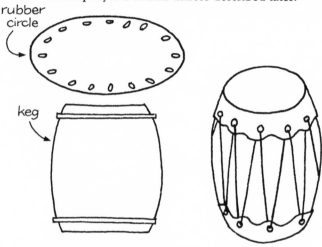

Smaller Drums

The simplest way to make a drum for each child is to use coffee cans. The plastic top provides some resonance; all that needs to be done is to make drumsticks. Sticks of the appropriate length are collected and a small amount of plasticine is molded around the end of the stick for the head. It can be covered with a square of sheeting and secured with a rubber band. The coffee-can drum itself can be painted with tempera by mixing a little liquid detergent into the paint, which will allow it to adhere to the metal surface.

Other frames for drums may be made from cheese boxes, oatmeal boxes, stone jars, buckets, or kettles. The drum head or covering for the drum can be made from oiled paper or closely woven fabric. It can be

[7]Directions for making this drum are adapted by permission of Association Press from BOOK OF INDIAN LIFE CRAFTS by Oscar V. Norbeck, New York, Tower Publications, 1970.

fastened with tacks, rubber bands, or lacings of twine or shoelaces.

Musical Rattlers

For one variety you will need some empty ribbon-spools—the kind gift-wrap ribbon is sold on. The spools should be about four inches long. You will also need sticks or dowels ten inches long. First decorate the spool with paints, felt-tip pens, or cutout designs. Then cut a small hole in one end of the spool. Place beans, pebbles, or grains of rice through the hole into the spool. Put white glue on one end of a stick or a dowel, push it into the spool, and press it firmly against the top.

Another rattle can be made with toilet-paper rolls and ten-inch-long sticks or dowels. Cut two pieces of crepe paper three and a half inches wide and eight inches long. Glue crepe paper around one end of the tube and let it dry. Tie the paper at one end with a piece of string, and cut a fringe at the end of the crepe paper. Put the beans into the other end of the cardboard roll. Then glue on the remaining strip of crepe paper and tie it with a string. Finally, cover the roll with colored paper. Punch a hole through the center of the roll and push the dowel through.

All of these instruments can be used to accompany the dances. If you try the movements out yourself as you are reading the directions for the dances, you will see how simple they are.

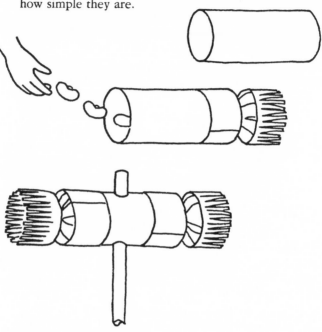

Snake Dance

In this dance, the dancers imitate the movement of a snake. They form a single line behind a leader, and their step is done to a steady drum beat. The left foot always remains slightly ahead of the right foot. First, step forward on left foot. Then, step forward on right foot, but keep left foot ahead. The hands are held in loose fists in front of the body. With each step, one hand is raised to chest level, while the other hand remains at the waist. Thus the hands and arms are moving along with the feet. The leader represents the head of the snake; the last one in line is the tail. At one point as the dance progresses, the "head" holds up his hands and yells. At that signal, everyone turns around, and the "head" becomes the tail and vice versa. Everyone follows the tail dancer until he holds up his hand and yells and the line reverses again.

Buffalo Dance

This dance is done in two parts. The first part is accompanied by "thunder drumming" in which a big drum is beat as fast as possible to imitate the roll of thunder. The second part is accompanied by a slow steady beat.

During the thunder drumming, the dancers scatter over the area, keeping their heads bent over like buffalo. They mill around like buffalo on the plain.

During the steady beat, the dancers jump up and down, hands on their waists, in time to the drum beat They land each time the drum beats.

The sequence of drumming is: a period of thunder drumming, followed by fourteen steady beats; thunder drumming, followed by twenty-eight steady beats; thunder drumming, then fourteen steady beats; thunder drumming, then twenty-eight steady beats.

Scout Dance

The dancers learn the basic toe step, which is not difficult. It is done in a four-beat sequence, with the hands on the waist throughout.

First, with the weight on the right foot, tap the ball of the left foot lightly on the ground just ahead of the right foot.

Second, move the left foot back next to the right foot, and shift the weight to the left foot.

Third, tap the ball of the right foot ahead of the left foot.

Fourth, place the right foot back in position and shift the weight to the right foot.

After the children have mastered this step, they can do the Scout Dance.

The dancers should be four feet apart in a line facing the audience. The first part is done to thunder drumming. The dancers kneel on one foot or squat and pretend to be looking for enemies. They pantomime various activities such as listening for enemy horses, checking their weapons, and so forth.

The second part is done to a medium beat of the drum.

Dancers, doing the toe step, move in a line toward the audience, stopping on the last beat of the drum. The two parts are repeated four times.[8]

Indian Songs

An excellent source for Indian music is *Songs and Stories of the North American Indians,* adapted by Paul Glass.[9] Three songs from the book that are particularly appropriate for use with young children are "I am Like a Bear," "I Sing for the Animals," and "The Waterbug Stands upon the Fish."

Indian Art

It would be helpful to have as many examples of Indian art as possible available to the children: clay bowls, woven rugs, sand paintings, dolls, beadwork. Reproductions and illustrations will serve if the real thing is not at hand. Many of the more advanced books about Indians are still useful for young children because of their pictures.

Totem Poles

A striking addition to your classroom during this time is a floor-to-ceiling totem pole made by the children. To form the base of the pole, collect empty coffee cans or juice cans and tape them one on top of the other. As the pole grows taller, you may wish to stabilize it by

[8]The dances are adapted by permission of G.P. Putnam's Sons from INDIAN DANCING AND COSTUMES, by William K. Powers, New York, Putnam, 1966, © 1966 by William K. Powers.
[9]New York, Grosset & Dunlap, 1968.

adding wet sand or heavy stones to the bottom can. If it becomes too unstable, several shorter poles can be made instead. When the pole is the desired height, cover it with brown wrapping paper. Put out on a table six-by-nine-inch pieces of black or brown construction paper. Each child uses colorful scraps of paper to construct a face on the paper. If the children have already seen pictures of totem poles, they will have many ideas. A few instructions can be given on how to make three-dimensional noses, ears, or arms. As the faces are completed, they are taped or glued to the totem pole, covering both the front and back.

An even larger version can be made by decorating cardboard boxes with paper cutouts and paint, and stacking them up to the desired heights.

Kachina Dolls

Here again, illustrations and examples are important. Many books have pictures of these southwest Indian dolls, and the children should have a chance to examine them before making their own. Paper towel roles make a good base for the body and head. Details can be added with felt-tip pens, paint, or scraps of paper. Arms and parts of the headress can be added by gluing scraps of paper to the tube.

Sand Painting

An approximation of colored sand can be obtained by mixing small amounts of tempera paint into white cornmeal (about one tablespoon of paint to two cups of cornmeal). The mixture is stirred until dry. The children are supplied with heavy construction paper or cardboard, white glue in small cups, and cotton swabs. Using the swabs they draw their picture in glue, and then sprinkle the "sand" over the glue, shaking off the excess. Only a small amount of glue should be spread at one time so that it does not dry up before being coated with "sand."

Paper Bag Masks

Pictures of masks used by Indians in their ceremonies will be very useful in giving children ideas for their own masks. After they are familiar with the pictures, a table can be supplied with paper bags, yarn, buttons, magic markers, and scraps of colored paper. The children may need help in marking the correct place for eyeholes and noseholes on large grocery bags, but otherwise they should be able to make the masks by themselves.

Paper Plate Masks

As a variation, children can decorate paper plates to represent animals or evil spirits, and then punch two holes in the sides of the rim opposite each other. Yarn is strung through the holes, and the mask may be tied around the child's head. The correct position for the eyeholes is marked, and they are cut out.

Indian Pottery

The Indian unit offers a good opportunity to have the children work with real clay. The coil method of making a bowl is simple to demonstrate and should result in a nice-looking bowl for the children to decorate and take home. The clay is worked and rolled into a thin coil. A flat, round piece of clay is formed for the base. Then the coil is wound upward in circles from the base, gradually building up the bowl until it is of the desired size. The finished bowl is smoothed with the fingers and then allowed to dry. If a kiln is available, the bowls can be fired and painted. If no kiln is available, they can be painted when dry.

Indian Food

The children will be interested in learning about the many native foods enjoyed by the Indians before European foods were introduced. Many of them are still familiar. An exhibit of pictures and samples of foods used by the Indians can be a basis for discussion of how their eating habits compared with ours, noting what things are now eaten by us as well and which are unfamiliar. These are some of the foods grown or harvested by North American Indians of different tribes:

corn (used for hominy, succotash, cornbread, cornmeal mush, tortillas, and tamales)

acorns (after leaching with water to remove their bitterness, they were ground into flour for bread or mush)

pecan and hickory nuts (both are known to us by
their Indian names)

grapes, strawberries, blackberries, gooseberries,
blueberries, and persimmons in their wild state. (In
the great plains, wild berries were mixed with
buffalo meat and fat to make pemmican, which
could be carried for long distances without spoil-
ing. Our modern "space sticks" and beef jerky are
similar.)

sunflowers

wild rice

Jerusalem artichokes

maple syrup and maple sugar

piñon nuts

squash and pumpkins

beans

The list may suggest many possibilities for foods you
can prepare in the classroom. *The Art of American
Indian Cooking*, by Yeffe Kimball and Jean Anderson,
is devoted to authentic Indian recipes adapted for
current use. The following two recipes were adapted
from their book.[10]

Squaw Bread

Yield: 3 flat, round loaves, about 10 inches in diameter, ½ inch thick

5 cups all-purpose flour	2 cups milk
2 tablespoons baking powder	1 tablespoon butter or margarine, melted
1 teaspoon salt	Cooking oil for frying bread

Sift 4 cups of the flour with the baking powder and
salt. Combine milk and melted butter. Place flour and
baking powder in a large bowl and add liquid ingredients a little at a time. When the 4 cups of flour have

[10]"Squaw Bread" and "Pumpkin Soup" adapted by permission of Doubleday
& Co., Inc. and McIntosh & Otis, Inc. from THE ART OF AMERICAN
INDIAN COOKING, New York, Doubleday, 1965, © 1965 by Yeffe
Kimball and Jean Anderson.

been worked into a soft dough with the milk, lightly flour a surface with part of the remaining cup of flour. Turn dough onto board and knead lightly, working in the rest of the flour. Divide dough into three parts. Shape each piece to fit the shape of the skillet you will be frying it in. An electric skillet or a cast-iron frying pan over a hot plate may be used. Pour enough cooking oil into the skillet to measure about a quarter of an inch deep. Heat the oil and brown the bread quickly, one to a skillet, until golden brown on both sides. Spread with jam or butter, cut into wedges, and serve.

Pumpkin Soup

Yield: 32 half-cup servings

2 cans (1 pound 13 ounces) pumpkin puree	2 teaspoons salt
	1 teaspoon marjoram
2 quarts milk	½ teaspoon cinnamon
¼ cup butter	½ teaspoon mace
¼ cup honey	Dash of pepper
¼ cup light brown sugar	4 cups orange juice

In a large saucepan heat the pumpkin puree, milk, butter, and honey together. Combine the light brown sugar, salt, marjoram, cinnamon, mace, and pepper, and stir them into the pumpkin-milk mixture. Heat slowly, stirring, to the simmering point. Do not boil. Add orange juice, a little at a time, stirring constantly. Serve hot.

You and Your Body

The unit I call "You and Your Body" gives children the chance to explore possibilities of their bodies and to learn about various physical aspects of how the body works. The development of self-image and of self-awareness is encouraged. Nutrition is also explored as an important way of keeping the body fit. The activities suggested in this chapter might take place over a three-week period, culminating in the cooking and eating of a complete meal in school.

To introduce children to thinking about themselves, ask the question, Who Am I? Have them bring in baby pictures and display them on a bulletin board. They can be compared with current pictures. Discuss with the children what they were like when they were babies: what they could and could not do, what they remember, how they are different now, what things they would like to do but still cannot do, and whether they will be able to do some of these things when they are older.

For each child, start a book entitled "About Me." Begin with the baby picture and add drawings or photos of the child's house, parents, friends, pets, and so forth. Some of the activities described below, such as weighing and measuring, and observation of self and others, can be incorporated into the book.

Weigh and measure each child. If possible, borrow the nurse's scale so that children can watch others being weighed. Or you might get the nurse to take children down to her office to be weighed. School nurses that I have worked with in various schools were always interested in helping out with this unit and were able to supply useful materials.

As the children are weighed, try to help them develop some skill in estimating what the weights will be. When they make their first predictions, they will probably be way off. But as the weighing progresses, some will be able to refine their guesses, using information previously noted: "If Mary weighs fifty pounds and Deborah is about her size, I'll guess fifty for her." A large graph, life-size, of the children's heights can be made by pasting strips of colored paper the correct lengths vertically on brown wrapping paper. This helps the children to see the differences in height as well as the numbers that are associated with the measurement. You can also make a comparative graph of weights, but only if you have no children whose weights are out of proportion to their age. They are aware of it enough without its being presented graphically for everyone to be amazed at.

Borrow a full-length mirror if you don't already have one. Have each child look at himself in the mirror for several minutes, then close his eyes and describe himself. A similar exercise can be done in pairs. Each child looks at his partner for several minutes, then closes his eyes and tries to describe as much as he can about the other child.

Sentences can be added to each child's book along the following lines:

I am _____ years old.
I have _____ hair.
I have _____ eyes.
I weigh _____ pounds.
I am _____ inches tall.
I like to eat _____.
These are my friends _____.

Illustrations or photographs can be added to the sentences to help remind the child when he tries to "read" them to himself.

A good book to read at this time is *I Like to Be Me* by Barbara Bel Geddes.[11] It is a fanciful exploration of all the things it would be fun to be (a balloon, the sun, etc.) but ends with the statement, "But most of all, I like to be me." Children may like to draw pictures of what they would like to be if they could be anything else in the world. The label on the picture can repeat the book's format so the child can be helped to "read" it. (I'd like to be a _____ so I could _____.)

To demonstrate how no two people are exactly alike, each child can make a fingerprint by rolling his finger on an inkpad and pressing it on a piece of paper. Use an overhead projector to compare the fingerprints to see how they differ from each other. This can lead to consideration of other ways people are different: skin color, hair color, foods they like to eat, what they like to do.

Ask the children to draw a picture of how they think they look inside. Collect the pictures and save them until after the unit is complete. Compare them with pictures drawn after the children have had a chance to examine models of parts of the body and look at pictures of skeletons and musculature.

Begin to explore with the children ways of using their

[11]New York: Viking Press, 1953.

bodies. Ask them to discover what sounds they can make with their bodies. What sounds can be made with just the arms, with just the hands, with the hands on different parts of the body, with the hands on things around the room, with just the feet, with just the mouth? What are some very soft sounds the body makes (breathing, heartbeat)?

Another chance to develop vocabulary comes as you ask children to show you different movements they can make with their bodies. Use words like swaying, jumping, stretching, twisting, bending, kicking, running, hopping.

Using the piano or recorded music, give the children time to do free movements to music, as suggested by the music (fast or slow, syncopated or steady, happy or sad.)

Suggesting things for them to imitate gives them a chance to use their bodies to express many things. Ask them to look like a rag doll, a falling leaf, a plant growing, a jack-in-the-box, spiders, children skating, popcorn popping. Ask them to show you how they feel when they're angry, sad, excited, scared, or happy.

The Ginn Company puts out an excellent series of "Dance-a-Story" records for young children. They tell a story on one side of the record, with a musical accompaniment, and the other side has only the music, without the words. After the children have listened to the story and danced to it several times, they can follow the music without the words. The records are very popular with children.

You can set up an activity center in the hall under the supervision of a parent or other volunteer. Here five or six children at a time can move through a series of physical activities. Among the activities might be:

Skipping up to a line and back
Hopping up to a line and back
Dropping and catching a ball a certain number of times
Rolling a ball back and forth to a partner
Going through a maze

For the maze, distribute cardboard boxes or big blocks in a course so that the children can crawl under things, step over things, step in and out of a box before proceeding, and so forth. If there is a physical education teacher in your school, he or she can help you by suggesting other good activities to be done in the hall.

A balance beam can be set up in a corner of the room or in the hall for children to walk on. If your school does not have one, you can make one by nailing a long two-by-four to two end-blocks. If you make several balance beams, you can set up a path for children to follow.

As the children explore their bodies and how they work, have them look at their hands. Compare these with animal "hands." How can monkeys use their hands? What about cats and dogs? Have the children list as many things as they can think of that they can do with their hands. Now choose a volunteer to have his thumb taped to his hand with masking tape. Without dislodging the tape, how many of the things on the list can he still do easily? Which are now impossible? Look for pictures of hands doing things to mount on a bulletin board.

The importance of caring for the body through adequate rest and cleanliness should be stressed. Discuss how combing the hair, brushing the teeth, washing the hands and face, bathing and getting a good night's sleep all help people to look and feel better. The children can learn the song "Wake Me" (see Chapter 9) and will enjoy making up additional verses.

Discuss with the children the importance of using their bodies to help make them strong. A few warm-up exercises can be done in the room every morning, and outdoor playtime should be included as often as weather permits.

Another opportunity for vocabulary development comes in learning the names of the parts of the body, both external and internal. There will be few children who don't know where their hands and arms are, but many will not know all of these parts: head, shoulder, neck, waist, hips, knees, ankles, feet, heel, toes, chin, cheeks, nose, eyes, forehead, elbow, wrist. The heart, lungs, stomach, bones, muscles, and blood vessels should also be discussed.

Trace the outline of a child's body on brown paper and cut it out. Draw in the features—the arms, legs, and so forth. Make large labels for different parts of the body (*HEAD, NECK, ARM*). As a group lesson, have children paste the labels in the proper places. Then make smaller dittoed models available to the children. Give them a sheet of paper with the various body parts listed. They can cut out the words and paste them on the model, using the larger model as a guide. This encourages visual discrimination and word recognition. The songs "Head, Shoulders, Knees and Toes" and "Put Your Finger in the Air" (see Chapter 9) both involve naming parts of the body.

To help the children learn about the insides of the body, it is extremely helpful to have available large models such as are commonly used in high school science classes. If at all possible, borrow some of these for the children to observe and handle during this unit. One year, I was able to borrow them from a friend who taught high school biology. Another year, the school nurse had them on loan from a manufacturer to examine for possible purchase, and she loaned them to us for the duration. It is quite a sight to see a group of children busily engaged in putting the organs back into a large torso: "No, the liver goes over here. . . . You have to put the lungs in this way or they won't fit."

If you know a doctor or one of the children's parents is a doctor, he or she may be able to provide you with old X rays. They give children an idea of what the skeleton looks like. Of course, if you are able to obtain a real one too, so much the better. Or, you can use smaller models and pictures to help the children visualize the bones inside them.

Have the children bring in animal bones from home. They can be boiled in detergent to clean them. Compare the sizes of different animal's bones: fish, chicken, cow. Perhaps the children have found animal bones in the woods which would be interesting to examine.

Have the children feel their bodies to see how many bones they can find. There are many small bones in the hand that are easily felt. Have them feel their neck, spine, ribs, legs. Where do they feel the biggest bones? the smallest? Has anyone ever broken a bone? What did they do to get it fixed? You will begin to get into nutrition here as the importance of milk for bone growth is stressed. Particularly for young children, milk is vital for proper development. This might be a good time to make a milk shake for everyone to enjoy. For thirty children, eight quarts of milk will supply everyone with one cup of milk shake. If you wish, you can use four quarts of whole milk and four quarts of reconstituted dry milk. Put in a blender one quart of milk at a time, using, for each quart of milk, any one of the following as flavoring: two very ripe bananas, one box frozen strawberries or raspberries defrosted, two large or three small, very ripe peaches. Blend until well mixed and serve. The anatomical song "Didn't It Rain" (see Chapter 9) is a good one to learn now.

There are several books about teeth that can be read to the children while bones are being studied. The books are listed in the bibliography at the end of this chapter. If you can get a large model of the teeth, you can demonstrate how to brush teeth properly. By smearing some peanut butter on an old comb and then using a toothbrush to get it off, children can see how effective a toothbrush can be in cleaning hard to reach places.

Children can collect magazine pictures of foods that help to make strong bones and teeth (citrus fruits, milk, cheese, and green, leafy vegetables). The importance of avoiding excess sugar should be stressed.

Read to the children *Hear Your Heart* by Paul Showers,[12] an introduction to the way the heart works, which is excellent for young children. Have a stethoscope available for children to listen with. Cardboard paper towel rolls can be used as well as actual stethoscopes. Also, a good substitute can be made with a small funnel, a plastic T or Y tube, and some rubber tubing. These should all be left for the children to experiment with in listening to their own hearts and to other children's.

Have the children locate the pulse in their neck. This is probably the easiest place for them to find the pulse, although you can show them how to find it at the wrist as well. Working with each child individually, you can take his pulse before and after he does some exercise, such as running in place for a short time. The results

---

[12]New York, Thomas Y. Crowell, 1968.

can be graphed for each individual child and for the class as a whole. For the individual graphs, prepare sheets with 10 squares across and 14 down, which will give you 140 squares. (You could achieve similar results by making a grid of 12 squares in each direction but the 10-square row allows you to emphasize counting by tens.) Most of the children's pulses will be well under 140 even after exercise, but there may be a few who will approach this limit. Printed above the grid is the sentence: My heart beats _____ times a minute. When you have measured the child's pulse, help him to color in the correct number of squares. He can record his normal pulse on one sheet and can record his pulse after running on a second sheet if he wishes. After all the children's pulses have been measured, a larger graph can be made by writing out each child's name and next to it pasting strips of graph paper cut to represent the number of heartbeats before and after running. Like the individual graph, the group graph gives the children a visual representation of the numbers, and a way of comparing them, though some may still have only a vague idea of what the larger numbers mean.

Children can feel their lungs expand as they take a deep breath. A further demonstration can be made using a balloon to show how air forces the lung to change shape as it passes in and out.

It is helpful to have some sort of microscope available to the children to aid them in understanding cells as the tiny building-blocks that make up all plant and animal tissue. The cells in a piece of onion skin are easily seen. The children can also look at samples of blood and hair through the microscope. Again, the high school science department may be able to loan you some slides that would be useful for the children to look at.

Developing the Five Senses

An awareness of the five senses can be developed along with other learnings about the body. Have the children close their eyes and imagine what it would be like to get along without them: what things would be impossible to do, what things would be difficult, what things might be the same.

Have available to the children microscopes, telescopes, magnifying glasses, binoculars, periscopes, and kaleidoscopes to examine and find out how each instrument affects one's perception of the world. (There are kaleidoscopes that have no bits of colored glass to form the designs but reflect whatever is being looked at and break it up into the familiar kaleidoscope patterns.)

Various visual memory games can be played which emphasize looking carefully and remembering. These are a few examples:

What Is Missing?

Put a collection of toys in front of several children, and let them scrutinize it for a few minutes. Cover it with a cloth, secretly remove one of the toys, and after removing the cloth, ask the children to identify what has been taken away. The game can be made more difficult, according to the abilities of the children, by using more objects and removing more than one object at a time.

Lost Child and Policeman

The children sit in a circle and one is chosen as policeman. The teacher begins as the mother describing her lost child to the policeman. The policeman, looking around the circle, finds the child fitting the description. Other children are chosen to play the policeman and mother.

Who Is Missing?

Children sit in a circle. One child is chosen to leave the room for a minute. While he is out, another child is picked to leave the circle and hide somewhere in the room. When the other child returns, he tries to guess who is missing. The game can be made more difficult by having the children exchange places in the circle after the missing child is hidden.

I Spy

One person sees something in the room and describes it by color: I spy something red. The other children look for red objects until they guess the one he was thinking of.

Hearing is another sense involved in many activities in the primary classroom. See Chapter 2, pp. 27–29, for suggested activities. Also, there are several books having to do with sounds and hearing that might be used at this point. They are listed in the bibliography at the end of the chapter.

The sense of touch can be incorporated into your program in many ways. A feel-me display can be set up in a convenient corner equipped with objects that are pleasant to feel, such as fur, feathers, smooth pebbles, glass paperweights, clay, ball bearings, buttons, sand, beads, velvet, and satin. The children can be encouraged to add their own contributions to the collection.

Discuss textures and other attributes with the children. What's the coldest thing you can think of? the hardest? the roughest? Word lists can be made under the headings THINGS THAT ARE COLD, THINGS THAT ARE SMOOTH, and so forth. Have available many scraps of materials and other things of different textures: nylon, velvet, satin, nylon net, lace, sandpaper, dried leaves, balloons, tinfoil, corrugated cardboard, candy papers. Put out shoe boxes and have the children suggest appropriate labels for the boxes for sorting the materials. After the boxes are labeled, put one or two samples in each box to help children in identifying what each sign represents. Then they can go to the table in their free time, feel the scraps, and put them in the appropriate box.

Make a PLEASE FEEL ME collage to put out in the hall for other children in the school to enjoy. Place a large square of brown wrapping paper on a table. Put out white glue and paste brushes. Each child can sketch a small area to fill in with the desired material. Some possibilities are sand, rice, small dried beans or peas, tiny buttons, scraps of material, and small twigs. After the collage has been completely filled in it can be displayed in the hall. Since you will be inviting children to handle it, it is probably safest to display it on a table rather than hanging on a wall, since the glue will hold better that way.

This would be a good time to get out the fingerpaints again, since fingerpainting involves so much tactile sensation.

Guessing objects by feeling them without being able to see them is an enjoyable game that can be played two ways. The first is to put numerous objects in a small laundry bag or pillowcase. The child is blindfolded, picks an object out, and tries to identify it by its shape and feel. For the second, cut out an armhole in each side of a cardboard box. Standing behind the box, the child puts his arms through the armholes and tries to identify an object that has been placed in the box. Some objects that might be used are a spool, a can opener, a plate, a toothbrush, a banana, a toy car, an eraser, an acorn, and a hammer.

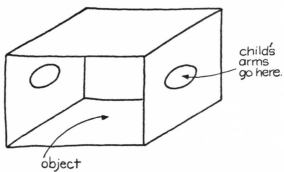

child's arms go here.

object

If you can find a Braille typewriter, type each child's name on a sheet of paper. When you give the children their names, and they have a chance to feel them, talk about the ways blind people use other senses to help them. Children may have seen a blind person tapping with his cane—using hearing and touch; and they may think of other examples.

To explore the sense of smell, a guessing game can be assembled. Put samples of some or all of the following substances in small jars: cinnamon, lemon peel, vanilla, onion, soap, vinegar, cocoa, banana, coffee, peanut butter, molasses, peppermint. Cover the jars with cloth. Working with one child at a time, blindfold him and have him sniff various jars and try to guess what is in each jar. The results can be graphed to show how many people guessed each substance. After the graph is complete, analyze it with the children. Which smell did most people guess? Which did fewest guess? Were there things which no one recognized? which everyone recognized?

A similar guessing game can be arranged to explore the sense of taste. In this case the substances would all have to be edible. Sugar, salt, chocolate, peanut butter, and banana are some that might be used. The results can be graphed the way the results of the smell test were. One variation of this game shows how dependent the sense of taste is on the sense of smell: have the children hold their noses while they taste. Compare the experience with the sensation of eating when you have a bad cold and your sinuses are stopped up.

Nutrition

As you talk about the body, you will be talking about what the body needs to keep it running well. Certain basic principles of nutrition can be established through activities and discussions. For example:

1. Good food makes people feel better, helps them grow, and gives them energy for work and play.

2. Food from each of the four basic food groups should be eaten every day.

    a. The milk group includes milk, cheese, ice cream, custard, yogurt, and buttermilk.

    b. Meats and meat substitutes include chicken, fish, steak, liver, turkey, eggs, dried beans and peas, and peanut butter.

    c. Vegetables and fruits generally known to the children are carrots, squash, spinach, lettuce, string beans, corn, beets, peas, citrus fruits, tomatoes, cantaloupes, apples, and grapes.

    d. With breads and cereals belong rice, spaghetti, and macaroni, as well as the various breadstuffs and hot and cold cereals.

3. Certain foods are better for us than others. We should avoid eating too much sugar and nutrition-

ally empty snack foods and try to include as many nourishing foods as possible.

More specific facts can be introduced according to the interest and ability of the children. You might discuss how various elements found in food are used in the body. Protein, found in eggs, meat, chicken, dairy products, and meat substitutes, helps build new cells and so helps build bones, muscles, blood, and skin. Calcium, found in dark green leafy vegetables and dairy products, helps build good bones and teeth. Iron, found in meat, dried beans, grains, and dried fruits, enables the blood to carry oxygen. Vitamin A, found in deep yellow and green vegetables, cheese, and butter, aids vision and helps to prevent infection. Vitamin C, found in citrus fruits and vegetables, helps wounds heal more quickly. The B vitamins, found in meats, grains, dried beans and other foods, help you to digest your food. Carbohydrates, found in breads and cereals, and fats help to provide energy and aid digestion.

Make many old magazines available for cutting out pictures of foods. The pictures can be used in a variety of classifying activities. In addition to helping them learn about foods, sorting and categorizing help to develop important math skills.

A chart can be made classifying various foods as FOODS FROM PLANTS, FOOD FROM ANIMALS. Foods from plants can be classified according to how they are grown: FOODS GROWN ABOVE THE GROUND, FOODS GROWN BELOW THE GROUND. A picture of an animal and its name can be accompanied by all the different food products coming from the animal. Pictures can be categorized into two groups: FOODS I LIKE, FOODS I DON'T LIKE. Or they can be sorted according to the four basic food groups. Charts can be made containing BREAKFAST FOODS, LUNCH FOODS, DINNER FOODS. A large chart of a plant naming edible parts (STEM, ROOT, LEAF, FLOWER, SEED, FRUIT) can be accompanied by pictures of kinds of food in each category: celery and asparagus (the stem); carrots and beets (the root); artichokes and broccoli (the flower); cabbage and lettuce (the leaf); beans and peas (the seed); and strawberries and apples (the fruit).

Have a box of toy food miniatures available on a table, and let children sort them according to some of these various categories.

The children can make up riddles about various foods. (It is orange. It grows under the ground. What is it?) These can be reproduced and bound into books for each child to take home.

In the hall or a corner of your room, set up a supermarket with the children, complete with buying and selling. Collect well-rinsed cans of vegetables, soups, and fruits, and empty cereal boxes, egg cartons, and milk cartons. For fresh fruits and vegetables, the children can make models of play dough or clay and paint them. The food can be arranged in the shelves according to the four basic food groups. Children may have noticed that in a grocery store, similar foods are grouped together. Ask at your local supermarket for old display signs and other materials. The people in charge will be glad to donate things they no longer need.

The children can help price the items in the classroom store. For ease in buying and making change, most items should be kept under ten cents. That is not very realistic, of course, and you may wish to sacrifice ease in handling money for a more lifelike price structure. Toy money and a make-believe cash register complete the store. The children can take turns being storekeeper.[13]

Give the children shopping lists with items from each of the four food groups. Have them buy the items at the store. Help them to make up their own shopping lists.

Collect pictures or samples of different ways a particular food is processed to help the children understand how much many foods change on their way from the farm to the table. For example, an ear of corn becomes cornflakes, cornmeal, corn muffins, or cornstarch. Milk can be turned into butter, cottage cheese, dry milk, or

[13]After interest in the supermarket wanes, the store can be converted into a beauty parlor, a barber shop, a bakery, a pet store, a garden shop, or a hardware store, with a few changes in props.

ice cream. The soybean can be made into milk, bean curd, or soy sauce.

To illustrate how drying works in preserving food, bring in several grapes and several raisins. Put the grapes in a dry place for a week. They will shrivel up until they begin to look like raisins. Meanwhile put the raisins in a cup of water. They will swell up until they look more like grapes.

Bring in samples of dried prunes and apricots. Give each child two pieces of each. Let the children soak one piece of each fruit in water, then compare its texture and taste with the unsoaked one.

Cut a fresh piece of apple and carrot and outline it on a piece of paper. Place them in the sun for a few days. Now compare the size and texture with the fresh one.

Children can do some processing of their own. Give three or four children an empty baby food jar and some heavy cream so they can make butter (see chapter 6).

Peanut butter can be easily made in the classroom. Put two cups of roasted peanuts into a blender. Grind the peanuts, adding a little peanut oil as necessary. In a few minutes, you will have fresh peanut butter. If the peanuts were not salted, add salt to taste. Both the peanut butter and the butter can be served on freshly made bread. (See chapter 6 for recipe.)

Before or after baking bread at school, it would be interesting to take a trip to a nearby bakery to see how bread and pastry is made in large quantity. After the visit, children can draw pictures of what they saw; the pictures can be bound into books for the class to look at. In addition, children can record on tape their impressions of the bakery, and the tapes can be made available at the listening station.

A toss game can be made for children to play by themselves. A large piece of oaktag (eighteen by twenty-four inches) is divided into sections. Pictures of foods that are good for you are pasted in some sections. Pictures of candy, potato chips, and other snack foods are pasted in other sections.

The card is placed on the floor. In order to score, children must toss a button or bottle cap onto the pictures of foods that are nourishing, not the candy or snacks.

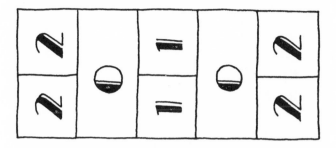

A fishing game can be set up along the same lines. A number of oaktag fish are cut out. Pictures of different foods are fastened to them with a paper clip. The child fishes with a string to which a magnet has been attached. The fish are scattered on the floor. He scores a point each time he picks up a fish with a good food on it.

A culminating activity for "You and Your Body" is the planning and cooking of a meal at school. The children can plan the meal, keeping the four basic food groups in mind. A shopping list is then made from the menu and a trip to the supermarket is made. To cut down on the cost, you may wish to ask parents to supply some of the items.

Before taking the children to the store, ask the manager if he will take the children behind the scenes at the store and show them produce being unpacked and meat being wrapped. He may even show them the meat locker, with its sides of beef hanging ready for cutting. Take photos or slides of the trip to be used later for stories. After they have been to the store, you can show them the pictures in *Supermarket* by Dolores Baugh.[14] In small groups, they can dictate their own stories to go with the pictures.

Children can make their own placemats for the meal. They can cut out breakfast or lunch foods and glue them to colored paper. Or they can draw their own pictures to decorate the mat. The children also help in preparing and serving the meal. My own experience

[14] New York, Noble & Noble (Chandler Reading Program), 1970.

has been that children are more appreciative of many foods when they have spent time learning about how the foods help the body work. Parents commented that children were eating more for breakfast at home after making breakfast in school.

Menus for Meals Prepared at School

Breakfast:

ORANGE JUICE — If you have an electric juicer, bring it to school so children can squeeze their own orange juice. Fresh juice can be mixed with frozen to cut down on the expense.

MILK — Should be available as a beverage and for cold cereal.

CORNFLAKES, or some other cold cereal, should be available for those who don't eat eggs, but you may find children eating both, so be sure to have plenty.

BLUEBERRY MUFFINS — Can be made from a mix to save time but it is more expensive to use a mix than to make them from scratch.

SCRAMBLED EGGS — Have several electric frying pans going so that everyone can be served at once.

Lunch:

ASSORTED SANDWICHES — If the children choose the kinds of sandwiches the most popular ones are likely to be tuna fish, peanut butter and/or jelly, and grilled cheese, all of which are easily prepared and inexpensive.

CARROT AND CELERY STICKS

MILK, FRUIT JUICE, OR COCOA

INSTANT PUDDING

Indians—Books
for Teachers

- Amiotte, Arthur, ART AND INDIAN CHILDREN OF THE DAKOTAS: AN INTRODUCTION TO ART AND OTHER IDEAS (Books 1–5), Aberdeen, South Dakota, Office of Educational Services, U.S. Dept of Interior, Bureau of Indian Affairs, 1982.

- Amon, Aline, TALKING HANDS: INDIAN SIGN LANGUAGE, New York, Doubleday, 1968.

- Baldwin, Gordon C., HOW THE INDIANS REALLY LIVED, New York, Putnam, 1967.

- Brindze, Ruth, THE STORY OF THE TOTEM POLE, New York, Vanguard, 1951.

- Cooke, David C. and Moyers, William, FAMOUS INDIAN TRIBES, New York, Random House, 1954.

- Fletcher, Sydney E., THE BIG BOOK OF INDIANS, New York, Grosset & Dunlap, 1950.

- Glass, Paul (comp.) SONGS AND STORIES OF THE NORTH AMERICAN INDIANS, New York, Grosset & Dunlap, 1968.

- Henry, Edna, NATIVE AMERICAN COOKBOOK, New York, J. Messner, 1983.

- Hofsinde, Robert, (Gray-Wolf), INDIAN GAMES AND CRAFTS, New York, Morrow, 1957.
  INDIAN MUSIC MAKERS, New York, Morrow, 1967.
  INDIAN PICTURE WRITING, New York, Morrow, 1959.
  INDIAN SIGN LANGUAGE, New York, Morrow, 1956.
  INDIANS AT HOME, New York, Morrow, 1964.
  INDIANS ON THE MOVE, New York, Morrow, 1970.

- Hunt, W. Ben, THE COMPLETE HOW-TO BOOK OF INDIAN CRAFT (Orig. title: BEN HUNT'S BIG INDIAN CRAFT BOOK), New York, Macmillan, 1973 (paper), 1969 (hardbound, orig. title).

- Kimball, Yeffe and Anderson, Jean, THE ART OF AMERICAN INDIAN COOKING, New York, Doubleday, 1965.

- La Farge, Oliver, THE AMERICAN INDIAN, Racine, Wisc., Western Publishing (Golden Press), 1960.

- Martini, Teri, THE TRUE BOOK OF INDIANS, Chicago, Childrens Press, 1954.

- Norbeck, Oscar V., BOOK OF INDIAN LIFE CRAFTS, New York, Tower Publications, 1970.

- Powers, William K., HERE IS YOUR HOBBY: INDIAN DANCING AND COSTUMES, New York, Putnam, 1966.

- Showers, Paul, INDIAN FESTIVALS, New York, Thomas Y. Crowell, 1969.

- Unis, Edwin, INDIANS, New York, Thomas Y. Crowell, 1959, rev. 1979.

Indians—Books for Children

- Baker, Betty, LITTLE RUNNER OF THE LONG-HOUSE, New York, Harper & Row, 1962.

- Beatty, Hetty B., LITTLE OWL INDIAN, Boston, Houghton Mifflin, 1951.

- Belting, Natalia, THE LONG TAILED BEAR AND OTHER INDIAN LEGENDS, Indianapolis, Bobbs-Merrill, 1961 and Eau Claire, Wisc., E. M. Hale, 1961.

- Beltz, George, BULL-BULL, THE INDIAN BOY, St. Louis, Bethany Press, 1963.

- Benchley, Nathaniel, RED FOX AND HIS CANOE, New York, Harper & Row, 1964.

- Brock, Emma L., ONE LITTLE INDIAN BOY, New York, Knopf, 1950.

- Clark, Ann Nolan, IN MY MOTHER'S HOUSE, New York, Viking Press, 1941.
LITTLE INDIAN BASKET MAKER, Chicago, Melmont, 1957.
LITTLE INDIAN POTTERY MAKER, Chicago, Melmont, 1955.

- Evatt, Harriet, YOU CAN'T KEEP A SQUIRREL ON THE GROUND, CHIPPEWA INDIAN LEGEND, Indianapolis, Bobbs-Merrill, 1961.

- Floethe, Louise L. and Floethe, Richard, THE IN-DIAN AND HIS PUEBLO, New York, Scribner, 1960.

- Friskey, Margaret, INDIAN TWO FEET AND HIS EAGLE FEATHER, Chicago, Childrens Press, 1967.
  INDIAN TWO FEET AND HIS HORSE, Chicago, Childrens Press, 1959.
  INDIAN TWO FEET AND THE WOLF CUBS, Chicago, Childrens Press, 1971.

- Hader, Berta and Hader, Elmer, THE MIGHTY HUNTER, New York, Macmillan, 1943.

- Hoff, Syd, LITTLE CHIEF, New York, Harper & Row, 1961.

- Martini, Teri, THE TRUE BOOK OF INDIANS, Chicago, Childrens Press, 1954.

- McGovern, Ann, LITTLE WOLF, New York, Abelard-Schuman, 1965.

- McGraw, Jessie Brewer, LITTLE ELK HUNTS BUFFALO, Camden, N.J., Thomas Nelson and Sons.
  PAINTED PONY RUNS AWAY, Camden, N.J., Thomas Nelson and Sons.

- Moon, Grace, ONE LITTLE INDIAN, Chicago, Whitman, 1967.

- Parish, Peggy, GOOD HUNTING LITTLE INDIAN, Reading, Mass., Addison-Wesley (Young Scott Books), 1962.

- Pine, Tillie S. and Levine, Joseph, THE INDIANS KNEW, New York, McGraw-Hill, 1957.

- Pistorius, Anna, WHAT INDIAN IS IT?, Chicago, Follett, 1956.

- Russell, Solveig P., INDIAN BIG AND INDIAN LITTLE, Indianapolis, Bobbs-Merrill, 1964.

- Williams, Frances, RED MOUSE, Austin, Texas, Steck-Vaughn, 1967.

You and Your Body—Books for Teachers

- Allison, Linda, BLOOD AND GUTS: A WORKING GUIDE TO YOUR OWN INSIDES, Boston, Little, Brown, 1976.

- Burns, Marilyn, GOOD FOR ME: ALL ABOUT FOOD IN 32 BITES, Boston, Little, Brown, 1978.

■ Wilt, Joy, TASTE AND SMELL: 40 TASTING AND SMELLING EXPERIENCES FOR CHILDREN, Waco, Texas, Creative Resources, 1978.

You and Your Body—Books for Children

■ Aliki, MY FIVE SENSES, New York, Thomas Y. Crowell, 1962, 1972 (paper).
MY HANDS, New York, Thomas Y. Crowell, 1962.

■ Balestrino, Philip, THE SKELETON INSIDE YOU, New York, Thomas Y. Crowell, 1971.

■ Banks, Marjorie, HOW FOODS ARE PRE-SERVED, Westchester, Ill., Benefic Press, 1963.

■ Baugh, Dolores and Pulsiver, Marjorie, SUPER-MARKET, New York, Noble & Noble, (Chandler Reading Program), 1970.

■ Bel Geddes, Barbara, I LIKE TO BE ME, New York, Viking Press, 1953.

■ Borten, Helen, DO YOU KNOW WHAT I KNOW?, New York, Abelard-Schuman, 1970.
DO YOU MOVE AS I DO?, New York, Abelard-Schuman, 1963.

■ Brenner, Barbara, FACES, New York, Dutton, 1970.
BODIES, New York, Dutton, 1973.

■ Brown, Margaret Wise, THE COUNTRY NOISY BOOK, New York, Harper & Row, 1940.
THE INDOOR NOISY BOOK, New York, Harper & Row, 1942.
THE SEASHORE NOISY BOOK, New York, Harper & Row, 1941.

■ Carle, Eric, PANCAKES, PANCAKES, New York, Knopf, 1970.

■ Cole, William, WHAT'S GOOD FOR A FOUR-YEAR-OLD?, New York, Holt Rinehart and Winston, 1967.
WHAT'S GOOD FOR A FIVE-YEAR-OLD?, New York, Holt Rinehart and Winston, 1969, 1971 (paper).

WHAT'S GOOD FOR A SIX-YEAR-OLD?, New York, Holt Rinehart and Winston, 1965, 1972 (paper).

- Felt, Sue, ROSA-TOO-LITTLE, New York, Doubleday, 1950.

- Goldin, Augusta R., STRAIGHT HAIR, CURLY HAIR, New York, Thomas Y. Crowell, 1966.

- Green, Mary M., IS IT HARD, IS IT EASY, Reading, Mass., Addison-Wesley (Young Scott Books), 1960.
WHOSE LITTLE RED JACKET, New York, Watts, 1965.
- Hoban, Russell, BREAD AND JAM FOR FRANCES, New York, Harper & Row, 1964; Eau Claire, Wisc., E. M. Hale, 1964; Scholastic Book Services (StarLine Books), 1969 (paper).

- King, Robin and Billie, JUST THE RIGHT SIZE, New York, Dutton, 1957.

- LeSieg, Theodore, THE EYE BOOK, New York, Random House, 1968.

- McGovern, Ann, TOO MUCH NOISE, New York, Houghton Mifflin, 1967.

- Schloat, G. Warren Jr., YOUR WONDERFUL TEETH, New York, Scribner, 1954.

- Showers, Paul, A DROP OF BLOOD, New York, Thomas Y. Crowell, 1967.
FIND OUT BY TOUCHING, New York, Thomas Y. Crowell, 1961.
FOLLOW YOUR NOSE, New York, Thomas Y. Crowell, 1963.
HEAR YOUR HEART, New York, Thomas Y. Crowell, 1968.
HOW MANY TEETH, New York, Thomas Y. Crowell, 1962.
LOOK AT YOUR EYES, New York, Thomas Y. Crowell, 1962.
USE YOUR BRAIN, New York, Thomas Y. Crowell, 1973.
YOUR SKIN AND MINE, New York, Thomas Y. Crowell, 1965.

- Teadorescu, Radu, KID FITNESS, New York, Seaview Books, 1979.

- Tudor, Tasha, FIRST DELIGHTS: A BOOK ABOUT THE FIVE SENSES, Bronx, N.Y., Platt & Munk, 1966 and Eau Claire, Wisc., E. M. Hale, 1966.

6

cooking
in the classroom

Cooking can be one of the most successful parts of a primary program. Children invariably love to do it and you will find many opportunities to integrate foods and cooking into your program. The development of science and math concepts is a part of every cooking experience, as children observe, smell, taste, and measure. In addition, reading over the recipe with the children before cooking, and giving out copies of the recipe for them to take home provides many language experiences and stimulates interest in reading and following written directions. Parents can become involved as volunteers in the cooking in the classroom, or at home when they use the recipes you send home to bake with their children.

The recipes that are included in this chapter have all been used with kindergarten children, and the children really did most of the work. It is very important that they be involved in *all* aspects of the project: greasing the pans, measuring the ingredients, breaking the eggs (have a few extras on hand!), putting things in the oven, and cleaning up. If you are not directing the activity yourself, be sure that your adult helper understands the importance of children's involvement. Many times it will be faster for the adult to do something instead of helping the child to do it, but except in emergencies, it should be avoided. The whole process can be a learning experience for the children, and they love every step of it, not just the end result.

When you are cooking with little children, safety is

extremely important, but it should never be used as an excuse not to involve the children in the project. The children must be supervised, though. To that end, only a few children at a time should take part. Parents are usually very willing to come in and help out, though there are many times when you will want to do it yourself. Care must be taken when a hot plate is set up that it is in a secluded place where it will not be knocked over. Cords must be carefully placed so no one trips and pulls over a hot dish. The same precautions you take when cooking at home are good ones to follow when working with children. Remember that when something starts to smell good, or make noises, or when anything interesting happens, the children will swarm to the spot. Be prepared so that everyone can have a chance to smell or taste or watch without crowding, and disasters can be avoided.

When planning a cooking project with the children, discussing the required ingredients is the first step. The discussion helps to develop vocabulary, not only of objects the children may be unfamiliar with (turnip, molasses), but also mathematical terminology used in measuring (cups, teaspoons, pounds). Either the children can be asked to bring the items in from home, which helps to involve the parents in the project (be sure school regulations permit it) or a trip to the store can be made. Math will be involved here in discussions of how much money is needed, how much is to be bought, what coins will be used, and so forth.

The Day You Cook

Have the recipe already printed on a large sheet of oaktag, perhaps with visual cues (pictures of three cups of flour, two cups of milk). Discuss with the whole class the recipe and the procedure to be followed: some children will mix the dough, some children will roll out the dough, everyone will decorate the cookies, and everyone will eat the cookies. Since with a large class it is not practical for every child to participate in every facet of one particular project, the children should understand what the options are. If you do a lot of cooking, everyone will have many chances to experience the different phases during the year.

After the recipe has been discussed with the whole group, the children choose which part of the project they want to work on, and then a small group goes over to begin cooking. The recipe is read once again, and ingredients are discussed and examined at first hand. Many opportunities arise for discussion of amounts and recognition of numerals. Emphasize counting and other math concepts at every turn: We've put in two tablespoons, so how many more do we need? This measuring cup holds one cup, but we only need a half-cup of milk. This bag of sugar weighs five pounds; how much will it weigh when we're finished? How many cookies did we put on that tray? How many spoons and cups do we need for the chocolate pudding? Because the experience is vivid and interesting to the children, they will absorb a great deal in an informal way.

Science concepts are also developed during the cooking. Children are encouraged to observe closely and talk about what they see. What happens when milk is added to the flour? What happens to egg whites when they are beaten? How does sugar feel and taste? Does salt feel different? Does it taste different? When batter is poured into the cake pan, it is liquid. What happens to it when it's baked? What happens to butter when it's heated? What makes cookies get larger in the oven? Children should be encouraged to observe, to make predictions, to estimate, to describe. Some projects lend themselves to a further development of science concepts. For example, when the class is making applesauce, talk about where the apples come from, how the tree grows, what different apples look like. Perhaps you can plant apple seeds and other fruit seeds in little pots and watch them grow.

Since cooking involves virtually all the senses, it is also a wonderful medium for developing language and self-expression. Encourage the children to talk about what they are doing: what it looks like, feels like, tastes like. When it is time to take out the cookies or the bread, be sure all the children have a chance to smell the wonderful aroma that fills the room near the oven. After the children have eaten, write down their comments on a big chart which can be posted somewhere in the room. After a marathon pancake-eating session, we recorded comments such as: "They taste good." "I like to eat pancakes." "They were round." "I turned mine over." The children were often able to "read" these simple and basic sentences back to the others with a little help. Sometimes you might ditto up sentences about a project and send them home.

It is a good idea to send a dittoed copy of the recipe home as well. After making something at school, children enjoy repeating the experience at home. Of course, not all mothers enjoy cooking, particularly with small "helpers" around, and cooking at school can be especially important for the children who have never done any cooking at home. But many mothers will be delighted to receive the recipes and follow through at home. One year in our classroom, at least three mothers began baking all the family bread after the bread recipe was sent home.

Cooking in the classroom can be a way not only of involving the home but of encouraging interaction among different classes. In one school a "bake shop" was set up to raise money for school projects. The kindergarten and first grade classes got together to make peanut butter Rice Krispie bars to sell. The project was done out in the hall between the two classrooms with supervision by mother volunteers. Since no cooking was involved, except for melting butter, it made a good hall project. As much as the different schedules allowed, first graders worked with kindergarten children in preparing the bars. At Thanksgiving time, we had a feast with the first grades for which food was cooperatively prepared. This kind of interaction offers opportunities for breaking away from the traditional isolation of classes within grade levels and the four walls of one classroom.

As often as possible, you should try to correlate cooking projects with a particular unit. For example, at the beginning of the year, you might have a short unit on apples. As part of the unit, take a trip to a nearby cider mill or orchard where you can purchase apples to take back to the classroom to make applesauce. If a trip is impossible, ask each child to bring in one apple. As a reminder, children can draw a picture of an apple, and print the word underneath if they wish. Children can sort pictures of apple trees at different seasons of the year into sequential order. They can examine different varieties of apples, comparing taste and appearance. They can collect pictures of different products made from apples.

As part of a unit on You and Your Body, which includes a study of nutrition, (see Chapter 5) you can make bread, peanut butter, and even cook a whole meal at school (breakfast for one class, lunch for the other). Children can be involved in planning the menu, making the shopping list, going to the store, and cooking and eating the meal.

Your equipment need not be elaborate. Many things can be made with only a hot plate or electric frying pan. With only a hot plate you can make jello, applesauce, popcorn, candy, soup, pancakes, scrambled eggs, and grilled cheese sandwiches. If your school does not have an oven which you can use, a miniature oven would be a good investment.

To stock your cooking corner at the beginning of the year, look for donations, ask parents to send things in, and scout thrift shops and garage sales. The following equipment is very useful in classroom cooking. Of course if you cannot obtain all of these items, you can bring them from home as needed, but it is much more convenient to have them on hand.

mixing bowls of various sizes

measuring spoons and cups

wooden spoons for mixing (they don't get hot and so are safer than metal spoons for children to use)

pancake turners

spatula

rubber scraper

pastry blender

rolling pin (the small cylindrical blocks that come with any kindergarten block set are easy for children to handle. You might reserve a couple for the cooking cupboard for this purpose.)

several cookie sheets

large cooking pot (for soup, applesauce, etc.)

several saucepans

several aluminum pie plates

13×9-inch pan

small bowls, such as plastic margarine container or cottage cheese tubs; they are useful for individual portions of frosting, etc.

plastic forks, knives, and spoons
paper plates and napkins
dishwashing liquid
assorted knives: a sharp one for adult use and
    several paring knives for children to use with
    supervision
eggbeater
ladle and other large metal spoons

In addition to the "hardware" it is also convenient to
keep certain staples on hand in the cupboard. Most
important are:

flour	confectioners sugar	cinnamon
(all-purpose)	salt	cooking oil
brown sugar	baking powder	
white sugar	vanilla	

With them on hand you will only need to get a few
items when you are ready to cook. In the places where
I taught, we were able to ask the parents for donations
of small amounts of things such as flour and sugar
Where school regulations do not permit that, you will
either have to buy cooking materials yourself, or ask
the school to fund you.

The rest of the chapter contains recipes suitable for use
in classroom cooking. Most of them have been tested
many times with kindergarten children.

Recipes—
Stone Soup

The well-known story "Stone Soup," by Marcia Brown
(New York, Scribner, 1947), is a great favorite of
young children. After you have read it to your class,
they will enjoy making soup more or less as the
soldiers make it in the book. You can plan a trip to the
grocery store or roadside market to buy vegetables, or
have each child bring one thing from home. Once you
have assembled the ingredients, they will need to be
cut up. Cutting is a difficult skill, and a mother can
supervise a few children at a time while the others are
doing other things. The adult may have to take over
the cutting at times. You can put some meat in the
soup if you like, but it will be quite delicious using
only vegetables.

1 large onion,
  chopped
2 carrots, chopped
2 ribs celery with
  leaves, chopped
½ cup butter or mar-
garine
Salt to taste
1 can tomatoes
  (1 pound 12 ounces)

2 quarts water
6 cups assorted cut up
  vegetables (cabbage,
  carrots, corn, pars-
  nips, potatoes, spin-
  ach, string beans,
  zucchini, etc., in any
  combination. More
  than 6 cups may be
  used.)

In a large kettle melt butter. Add onion, carrots, and celery and cook over low heat for 5 minutes, until tender. Add tomatoes, water, and cut up vegetables. Simmer covered 30 minutes. Season to taste and serve.

Gingerbread Men

This project was always done as part of a unit on the story of the Gingerbread Man, which included reading different versions of the story, acting it out, making and using stick puppets and flannel board cutouts, and making illustrations for the story. One year I tried having the children make their own patterns for the gingerbread men, but I found it too unwieldy. The children had difficulty cutting around the patterns on the dough, and often the arms were too thin to survive. Older children could probably do it, but we used cookie cutters to make the men.

This is a two-day project if it is done as part of a half-day program. The dough is mixed and the cookies cut out and baked one day, and then decorated the following day.

Yield: 32 gingerbread men, 4 to 5 inches each

½ cup butter or mar-
  garine
1 cup white or brown
  sugar
1 cup dark molasses
7 cups all-purpose flour
2 teaspoons baking soda

2 teaspoons ginger
1 teaspoon cinnamon
1 teaspoon salt
½ teaspoon ground
  cloves
½ cup water

In a large bowl blend butter and sugar together until smooth. Beat in molasses. Combine dry ingredients and add to butter mixture alternately with water. The last bit of flour may have to be worked in by hand, as the batter will be stiff. Roll out dough on clean floured surface to ¼-inch thickness. Cut out men with cookie cutter and place on greased baking sheet. Bake in 350°F. oven 8 minutes, until dough springs back when pressed lightly with finger. Remove from sheet and cool on racks.

For decorating have available at a table small bowls of raisins, chocolate chips, cinnamon candies, colored sugar, and confectioners sugar frosting (confectioners sugar mixed with water until it is of spreading consistency).

Yeast Bread

Yield: 30 individual loaves

6 cups warm water	15 – 18 cups all-purpose flour
3 packages yeast	(one 5- pound bag
3 cups nonfat dry	and part of
skim milk	another)
½ cup sugar	30 6½- or 7-ounce
6 tablespoons salad oil	tuna fish cans for
3 teaspoons salt	baking the individual
	loaves

FIRST DAY

Pour warm (not hot) water into very large bowl. Sprinkle yeast over surface of water. Add dry skim milk, sugar, salad oil, and salt. Stir until yeast is dissolved.

Add 13 – 15 cups flour, gradually mixing well. Sprinkle one cup of flour onto clean table top, empty dough onto table, using spatula to scrape bowl. Knead dough 10 minutes, until smooth and elastic, adding flour as necessary to keep dough from sticking to hands or table. (Amount of flour needed will vary with age of flour, humidity, etc., so you will have to experiment.) Dough may now be stored overnight in refrigerator. Use two or three large plastic bags, one inside the other. They should have a capacity of twice the volume of the dough, which will expand in the refrigerator. You can divide the dough into smaller quantities and use smaller bags if you wish. Place dough in bags, fasten securely, and leave in refrigerator overnight.

SECOND DAY

As soon as you get to school, remove the dough from the refrigerator and put it in a warm place. By the time the children are ready to work with it, the dough will have warmed sufficiently. Empty it onto a table and divide it into portions for kneading. Each child should receive a piece a little smaller than a tennis ball. After children have kneaded and shaped the dough, they should grease their tuna fish cans with butter or margarine and place the dough in the cans. Put the cans in a warm place (near a radiator or in a sunny window) until the dough has nearly doubled in size. It should take about 30 or 45 minutes. Bake in 350°F. oven 15 to 20 minutes, until deep golden brown. Remove from pans and let cool.

Butter

You may wish to make butter to go with the bread. Let heavy cream warm to room temperature. Pour a few tablespoons into each of several baby food jars. Screw caps securely. Let children take turns shaking jars until buttermilk separates from butter. Pour off buttermilk and scrape butter into a dish. Wash butter gently with cold water, working it with a wooden spoon. Add salt to taste and refrigerate if it is not to be used immediately.

Individual
Pizzas

The bread recipe just given can also be used as the basis for making individual pizzas. (If you wish to simplify the project considerably, you can use refrigerated biscuits and have each child flatten one into a round.) Proceed with the bread recipe to the point where each child receives his piece of dough. Then each child flattens his dough and smooths it into a circle 4 inches in diameter. Put small plastic dishes of tomato sauce and grated cheese on the cooking table, and have children spread their dough with 1 or 2 tablespoons of sauce, then sprinkle it with several tablespoons of grated cheese. Place pizzas on greased cookie sheets and bake in 425°F. oven 20 minutes, until cheese is melted and edges of dough are golden brown.

Decorated Cookies

For Halloween, Christmas, etc.

Yield: About 5 dozen cookies

¾ cup butter or margarine
¾ cup sugar
3 eggs

3¾ cups all-purpose flour
3 teaspoons baking powder
1½ teaspoons vanilla

In a large bowl cream butter and sugar. Beat in eggs, then add dry ingredients and vanilla. Blend well. Chill for 1 hour. Roll out dough to ⅛-inch thickness. Cut out into desired shapes. Place on greased cookie sheet. Bake in 350° F. oven 7 to 10 minutes, until dough springs back when pressed lightly with finger. This will take one half-day session.

On the next day, have children make frosting. Give each child a small plastic bowl, such as a margarine tub. Place ¼ cup confectioners sugar in bowl. Slowly add water, stirring until the frosting is of spreading consistency. Add food coloring as desired. Give each child a plastic knife and two cookies (or more, depending on how many you have) to decorate. Raisins and chocolate chips can be used for decorating Halloween pumpkin cookies, colored sugar and candies for Christmas cookies, etc.

Potato Pancakes

These can be made during the Hanukkah holiday.

Yield: 30 small pancakes

3 eggs
1 teaspoon salt
1 tablespoon onion, grated

6 cups raw potato, grated (can be done in blender)
All-purpose flour
Oil for frying

In a mixing bowl beat eggs until light, add salt, onion, and grated potato. Stir in flour, a tablespoon at a time, to make batter thick enough to pour slowly. Drop by spoonfuls into hot oil and brown slowly on both sides. Serve with applesauce.

Foods for a Thanksgiving Feast

In conjunction with a unit on Indians these recipes can be used to plan a feast based primarily on native American foods: cranberries, pumpkin, and corn. The recipes should serve one class of thirty children. If you are making them in cooperation with another class, you can expand them as needed.

Popcorn

Two and a half cups of kernels should give you about 5 quarts of popped corn. Allowing for some that will burn, some that fail to pop, and some that mysteriously disappear along the way, 2½ cups give you enough for 30 half-cup servings.

Corn Muffins

Yield: 36 small muffins

¾ cup all-purpose flour	2¼ cups cornmeal
3 tablespoons sugar	1¼ cups milk
3 teaspoons baking powder	2 eggs, beaten
1 teaspoon salt	¼ cup butter or margarine, melted

In a large bowl sift together flour, sugar, baking powder, and salt. Add cornmeal and mix well. In another bowl combine milk, eggs, and melted butter. Pour liquid ingredients into dry ingredients. Mix quickly. Pour into small muffin pans or gem pans. Bake in 425° F. oven 25 minutes.

Cranberry-Orange Relish

Yield: 5 cups relish

Children love to make this dish, but not too many of them like to eat it. It is a favorite with adults, however, so leftovers won't be a problem. You need an old-fashioned meat grinder to grind the fruit. Children love to make the grinder work.

4 cups cranberries (1-pound box)
2 oranges with rind
2 cups sugar

Grind cranberries. Cut up oranges and grind. Stir in sugar. Refrigerate until needed.

Cranberry Sauce

This is fun to make because of the way the cranberries start to pop as they cook. The children like to watch this, but keep them a safe distance away as the cranberries can "spit."

2 cups water
2 cups sugar
4 cups cranberries (1-pound box)

In a large saucepan combine water and sugar. Boil 5 minutes. Add washed cranberries and boil until berries stop popping (about 5 minutes). Chill. Serve cold.

Pumpkin Cookies

Yield: 4 dozen cookies

½ cup shortening
1 cup brown sugar
¼ cup granulated sugar
2 eggs, slightly beaten
2 cups canned pumpkin
½ teaspoon salt
½ teaspoon cinnamon
½ teaspoon nutmeg
½ teaspoon ginger
2½ cups all-purpose flour
4 teaspoons baking powder
1 cup raisins
1 teaspoon vanilla

In a large bowl cream shortening and sugars. Add eggs and pumpkin to creamed mixture. Add salt and spice and mix well. Sift together flour and baking powder and add raisins. Add to first mixture and mix well. Add vanilla. Drop by teaspoonfuls onto greased cookie sheet. Bake in 375° F. oven 20 minutes.

Two other recipes connected with Indian culture are given in Chapter 5, in the unit on Indians (see pp. 107). They are authentic Indian recipes, and you might like to include them in a feast.

Valentine Cake

Using your favorite cake recipe or a packaged mix, prepare batter for a two-layer cake. Pour batter into one 8- or 9-inch layer pan and one 8- or 9-inch square pan. Be sure that both pans are the same measurement. Bake as directed. When cakes have been baked and cooled, remove from pan. Have ready large plate or cookie sheet on which to assemble cake. Place square layer on tray. Cut round layer into two semicircles. Lay each half-circle along one edge of square layer to form a heart. Frost with prepared frosting or use the following recipe:

Frosting

4 cups confectioners sugar, sifted
6 tablespoons butter, softened
3 teaspoons vanilla
½ teaspoon salt

In a large bowl add sifted sugar gradually to softened butter. Blend until creamy. Add vanilla and salt. Tint with red food coloring if a pink shade is desired. If frosting is too thick, add a little milk or water; if too thin, add more sugar. Frost the cake and decorate it with candy hearts.

Easy Peanut Butter Cookies

Yield: About 60 cookies

3 cups creamy peanut butter
3 cups sugar
1½ cups salted peanuts
3 eggs
2 teaspoons vanilla

In a large bowl combine all ingredients and blend until smooth. Have each child roll balls of the mixture 1 inch in diameter. Have him place balls 1 inch apart on ungreased cookie sheet, putting his thumb in middle of each cookie to make indentation, then placing a few salted peanuts in each hole. Bake in 300° F. oven 15 to 20 minutes, until light brown.

Irish Soda Bread

This is a great recipe for young children to make: it's easy, fun to make, and delicious. Make it for St. Patrick's day or any time you want a quick baking project. The basic recipe makes one 9-inch pie plate of bread. If you want generous servings, cut the "pie" into eighths. You can cut it into smaller pieces and get 12 or even 16 per pie. Double and triple recipes are given so you can decide how many pieces you want and what size, and you can go from there.

one pie plate	two pie plates	three pie plates	
2	4	6	cups all-purpose flour, sifted
1	2	3	tablespoons sugar
½	1	1½	teaspoons baking soda
½	1	1½	teaspoons salt
3	6	9	tablespoons butter or margarine
½	1	1½	cups raisins
2	4	6	teaspoons carraway seeds
1	2	3	cups buttermilk

In a large bowl sift together flour, sugar, baking soda, and salt. Cut in butter with pastry blender. Add remaining ingredients. Mix thoroughly. Have children grease their hands before handling dough. Place dough in greased 9-inch pie plate. Pat into shape to fill pan, rounding top slightly. Bake in 350° F. oven 30 minutes, until golden brown. Serve hot, cut in wedges, with butter.

Easy Sesame Rolls

Yield: 32 rolls

4 packages refrigerator crescent rolls (8 rolls in a package)
2 cups milk
Large box sesame seeds

Open rolls. Spread out on wax paper. Separate rolls. Have each child roll up his own roll, starting with the wide end. Place rolls on cookie pan 1 inch apart. Sprinkle several teaspoons of milk on each roll. Sprinkle with sesame seeds. Bake in 375° F. oven 10 to 13 minutes.

Sugar Drop Cookies

Yield: About 60 cookies

2½ cups all-purpose flour	1 cup sugar
1½ teaspoons baking powder	¾ cup cooking oil
	2 eggs, lightly beaten
1 teaspoon cinnamon	1 teaspoon vanilla
¾ teaspoon salt	Granulated sugar for dipping

In a large bowl combine flour, baking powder, cinnamon, and salt. In another bowl combine sugar and oil, then add eggs and vanilla. Stir in flour mixture, blending well. Form into small balls and dip in granulated sugar. Place on lightly greased cookie sheet. Bake in 375° F. oven 10 to 12 minutes, until cookies spring back when pressed lightly with finger.

Quick Cake

Yield: 32 pieces of cake

2½ cups all-purpose flour
2 teaspoons baking soda
1 teaspoon salt
1 cup brown sugar, firmly packed
2 eggs
½ cup soft butter or margarine
1 can (1 pound) fruit cocktail, undrained
½ cup chocolate chips
½ cup chopped nuts

Grease and flour bottom of 13×9×2-inch pan. In a large bowl combine flour, baking soda, salt, brown sugar, eggs, butter, and fruit cocktail. Mix thoroughly. Then beat by hand or with an electric mixer at medium speed for 2 minutes. Pour batter into pan. Sprinkle with chocolate chips and nuts. Bake in 350° F. oven 40 minutes, until cake springs back when pressed lightly with finger or tester comes out clean.

Chocolate Peanut Clusters

Yield: 48 candies

1 pound milk chocolate
1 can (15 ounces) condensed milk
2 cups shelled peanuts or other nuts or raisins

In top of double boiler melt chocolate over hot water. Remove from heat. Stir in condensed milk and nuts or raisins. Be sure nuts are well covered with chocolate. Drop teaspoonfuls onto buttered cookie sheet and refrigerate several hours or overnight.

Oatmeal Cookie Mix

This is handy to mix up and keep on hand. Refrigerated, it will keep almost indefinitely. If you are keeping it in a cupboard, it is best to use it within six weeks.

Yield: 12 cups of mix

4 cups all-purpose flour, sifted	2 teaspoons baking soda
2½ cups granulated sugar	1 cup brown sugar, packed
3 teaspoons salt	2 cups shortening
	4 cups rolled oats, quick or regular

Sift flour, granulated sugar, salt, and baking soda into a large mixing bowl. Add brown sugar. Cut in shortening with pastry blender until mixture resembles fine crumbs. Stir in oats. Store in airtight container. Use in following recipe:

Oatmeal Cookies

Yield: About 3 dozen cookies

3 cups oatmeal cookie mix	1 egg
¼ cup milk	2 teaspoons vanilla

Place cookie mix in bowl. In another bowl combine milk, egg, and vanilla, beat well, and add to cookie mix. Mix thoroughly. Drop level teaspoonfuls of mixture 2 inches apart onto lightly greased cookie sheet. Bake in 350° F. oven 10 minutes, until golden brown. Cool on wire rack.

Fast Oatmeal Cookies

Here is a good, easy recipe for times when you need a large quantity of cookies.

Yield: 14 dozen (can easily be halved)

6 cups rolled oats
3 cups all-purpose flour, sifted
3 cups brown sugar, packed
3 cups butter or margarine
1 tablespoon baking soda
Granulated sugar for dipping

Place oats, flour, brown sugar, butter, and baking soda in large bowl and mash, squeeze, and knead with the hands until everything is thoroughly mixed. Form dough into small balls and place on ungreased cookie sheet. Butter the bottom of a small glass, dip in granulated sugar, and flatten the cookies. Bake in 350° F. oven 10 to 12 minutes, until crispy. Cool on the cookie sheet for a few minutes before removing.

Magic Cookie Bars

Yield: 30 bars 1½ × 2 inches

½ cup butter or margarine, melted
1½ cups graham cracker crumbs
1 cup chopped walnuts
1 cup chocolate chips (6-ounce package)
1⅓ cups flaked coconut (3½-ounce can)
1⅓ cups condensed milk (15-ounce can)

Pour melted butter onto bottom of 13×9×2-inch pan. Sprinkle crumbs evenly over butter. Sprinkle chopped nuts evenly over crumbs. Sprinkle chocolate chips over nuts. Sprinkle coconut over chips. Pour condensed milk over all. Bake in a 350° F. oven 25 minutes, until lightly browned. Cool in pan 15 minutes. Cut into bars.

Peanut Rice Krispie Bars

no baking

Yield: 32 2-inch squares

6 cups Rice Krispies
2 cups peanut butter

2 cups confectioners sugar
½ cup butter, melted

Mix all ingredients well with hands. Spread into two greased 8-inch square pans. Chill. Cut into bars.

Breadsticks

Yield: 32 breadsticks

4 packages refrigerator biscuits
1 cup butter or margarine
Large box poppy or sesame seeds

In large jelly roll pan melt butter. Separate biscuits. Roll each biscuit into 8-inch stick. Place sticks in melted butter, rolling as necessary to coat each stick thoroughly. Sprinkle with seeds. Bake in 450° F. oven 10 minutes. Let them stay in pan for 2 minutes after removing from oven so they can soak up more butter.

Applesauce

Yield: 30 small servings

30 large apples, cored and cut up (allow 1 apple per child)
2½ cups water
1½ cups sugar, or to taste, depending on sweetness of apples
2 teaspoons cinnamon

Place apples and water in large kettle. Simmer until apples are very soft. Stir in remaining ingredients. This will take all of one half-day session; applesauce will be completed next day. Refrigerate the mixture overnight. On the following day, let children take turns putting applesauce through a Foley food mill. Put into paper cups.

Chocolate Pudding

Yield: 32 half-cup servings

4 quarts milk
3 cups sugar
2 cups cocoa
1½ cups cornstarch

2 teaspoons salt
4 teaspoons vanilla
½ cup butter or margarine

In a saucepan mix together the milk, sugar, cocoa, cornstarch, and salt. Cook, stirring constantly, until mixture boils. Remove from heat; mix in vanilla and butter. Pour into cups.

Books for Teachers

- Ferreira, Nancy J., THE MOTHER AND CHILD COOKBOOK: AN INTRODUCTION TO EDUCATIONAL COOKING, Menlo Park, Calif., Pacific Coast Publishers, 1969.
  This book contains many recipes plus discussions of how cooking helps the child's development in many areas and tips on organizing a cooking program.

- Goodwin, Mary T., and Pollen, Gerri, CREATIVE FOOD EXPERIENCES FOR CHILDREN, Washington, D.C., Center for Science in the Public Interest, 1974.

Books for Children

- Croft, Karen, THE GOOD FOR ME COOKBOOK, San Francisco, Rand E. Research Assoc., 1971.

- dePaola, Tomie, THE POPCORN BOOK, New York, Scholastic, 1978.

- MacGregor, Carol, THE STORY COOKBOOK, New York, Doubleday, 1959.

- Mandry, Kathy, HOW TO MAKE ELEPHANT BREAD, New York, Pantheon, 1971.
  A collection of snacks with silly names; no cooking is involved.

7
plants and animals in the classroom

Plants and animals bring the fascination of growing things into your classroom. Many rewarding experiences are available to your children as they grow their own plants from seeds, learn about growth and reproduction, weigh and measure classroom pets, learn about differing habitats and ways of adapting, and take on the responsibility of caring for the classroom flora and fauna. The wonders of nature will unfold in your room as cocoons open, baby chicks hatch, pumpkin seeds show their first green tips above the soil, and a sprouted sweet potato covers the countertop with greenery.

Planting Seeds, Cuttings, and Bulbs

In the fall, seeds are everywhere as various weeds and grasses ripen and let their seeds fall. Children may unwittingly be carriers for some seeds as they brush past them on their way to school. Acorns and other nuts are falling. This is a good time to talk about how plants reproduce themselves and to collect as many samples as you can.

Fall is also a good time for planting bulbs. Is there an area around your school that could use some spring color? One year we were given permission to plant daffodils in front of the school building. Working with another kindergarten class, we dug up the area to be planted. Since it was close to our classrooms, we let the children go out a few at a time and work with child-sized rakes and shovels. It was a good outlet for excess energy and a very popular activity.

After the soil was well cultivated, we mixed in bone meal and peat moss supplied by parents. Then each child brought in twenty-five cents to buy a bulb. We toured a neighboring nursery and saw many beautiful plants. Then each child looked through bins full of bulbs and chose one he liked from the pictures above each bin. Each child paid for his bulb himself and carried it back to the school. The nursery also gave us a bag of crocus bulbs, so we gave each child a bulb to take home and plant.

The next day, a few children at a time went out to plant the bulbs. They used a ruler to measure the hole they dug to see if it was the proper depth. After all the bulbs were planted, they were thoroughly watered. The next spring, the display of daffodils in front of the school was beautiful, and doubly exciting for the children who had planted them and waited all winter for them to come up.

In addition to outdoor plantings, seeds of common plants can be planted in the classroom. Green beans are excellent for this purpose because they come up very quickly and form large, sturdy plants. You might also want to try marigolds or some other easily grown flower. Radishes are another quickly grown crop; you can plant them at school and harvest them in about three weeks. I found that used half-pint milk cartons from the school lunchroom with one or two drainage holes punched in the bottom were cheap and readily available potting containers.

For the initial experience of planting, you may want to ask a mother to come in to help the children. The children write their names and the names of their plants on a strip of masking tape that is fastened to the milk carton. Then they fill the carton with soil, make a hole in the soil for the seeds, and plant them. The mother can make sure that they do not plant the seed too deep. Once they have learned this, they can do planting on their own. The pots are watered carefully and placed in the window. In the spring, when the ground warms up, many parents will be planting backyard gardens. You may want to do this planting with your children then, so they can take their new plants home and plant them outdoors. For children who live in apartments, the plants should be repotted in large containers with adequate drainage and placed on a fire escape or window sill. Bush beans, cherry tomatoes, radishes and lettuce are all readily grown in containers if they receive plenty of light and water.

Once the children have learned how to plant, a large box of dirt can be left out with several packets of seeds, with paper cups and milk cartons for containers. (You can recycle the used juice cups for this purpose by having the children rinse them out after using, and storing them in a designated place.) The children can be free to plant as many seeds as they want, and you will find many taking advantage of the opportunity.

There are many opportunities to tell stories and make pictures, charts, and graphs about the growing plants. A chart can show the date the seed was planted, the date the first shoot appeared, the date of the first leaf, and so forth. Over a period of days, measurements of the new plant's height can be made and incorporated into a graph. Pictures of what the children did and what happened can be drawn and the children can dictate stories to accompany them. Lotto games that feature pictures and names of common flowers and vegetables can be played. The electric board or pegboard can be set up with matching games that use pictures from seed catalogs and the names of the plants.

In the fall, plant a few acorns and keep them in a cool place. If you are lucky, they will sprout in a few months. Orange and grapefruit seeds from the children's breakfast can be washed off and planted two inches deep in good potting soil in a small pot. While these seedlings will never bear fruit, they will make beautiful little green plants.

Avocado seeds are particularly interesting to the children because of their size. If you have never had any luck with the traditional way of planting them (sticking toothpicks into the seed and suspending it in a glass of water until the roots form), try the following method: wrap the seed in damp paper toweling and put it in a screw-top jar. Tighten the top well and put the jar away in a warm dark place. Check it in three or four weeks to see if the roots have started to form. If they have, plant the seed root side down in a pot of good soil. Do not entirely cover the seed with dirt; leave about a third of it showing. Place it in a sunny window and keep it watered. Before long the seed will split and the sprout will appear from within the seed.

Sweet potatoes make absolutely beautiful trailing vines. Stick toothpicks into the sweet potato and insert it into a glass of water, so that the potato is half submerged. If you can find a potato in the store that has already begun to sprout, the process will take less time. These vines will grow almost indefinitely as long as you keep the water clean.

Seeds from your Halloween pumpkin will sprout very readily, but you may prefer to wait until spring when the plants can be transplanted to the children's home gardens. Be sure to save the seeds even if you do not plan to plant them. They can be toasted gently in a moderate oven until fragrant, and the children will enjoy eating them.

Slice the top from a pineapple, leaving about one inch of flesh below the leaves. Let it dry for a day before inserting it in wet sand. It will begin to grow new leaves from its crown. Once it has rooted, repot it in good soil and keep it in a sunny window.

A pretty little garden can be made in a shallow dish or tray by filling it with damp sand and then putting in carrot tops, beet tops, turnip tops, and radish tops. Just slice off the vegetable about one-half inch from the top. These will sprout pale leafy greenery in no time. The garden will keep quite well if the sand is kept damp, but not wet, all the time.

Make new plants from cuttings of other plants. Many plants will form roots readily from cuttings placed in glasses of water. Among these plants are the philodendrons, English ivy, wandering Jew, and oleander. Other plants can be rooted if three- to four-inch cuttings are made and inserted into a small flower pot filled with rather sandy soil. These plants include coleus, geranium, and impatiens, as well as philodendron and ivy. Perhaps the most fascinating for children are the plants which will form miniature plantlets from a leaf of the parent plant: African violets, rex begonias, and gloxinia.

African violets can be rooted by placing a leaf-stem in a glass of water. Fill the glass with water and cover it with a piece of wax paper held in place with a rubber band. Poke a hole in the middle of the wax paper and push the stem through and into the water so that it is about one inch under water. Keep it in a warm, light place but not in direct sunlight. Roots will appear in several weeks. In about two months, tiny little leaves will cluster at the base of the larger leaf. The cutting can be planted in soil at any time after the roots appear.

To reproduce a geranium, cut a healthy stem about three or four inches long. Make the cut just below the leaf joint. Insert the stem into either a clay pot filled with moist sand or a glass of water. The children will be able to watch the development of roots better in the glass. The plants should be planted in sandy soil when the roots are three inches long.

In the early spring, branches of forsythia and other flowering trees and shrubs can be forced to bloom indoors. Cut the branches from forsythia, apple, or other trees several weeks before they would normally bloom outside and put them in water. Pussy willows may also be forced to open in this way. They root extremely quickly in water, so after you have enjoyed them inside, plant a few pussy willow branches somewhere around the school.

An interesting growing project for the classroom involves turning large turnips or rutabagas into flower pots. Put out several large turnips or rutabagas (at least four inches in diameter) along with some metal spoons for the children to use in hollowing them out. They should leave a shell of about one inch in thickness all the way around. Once they are hollowed out, fill them with soil and plant several morning glory seeds in each one. Push three small nails around the top edge and suspend the rutabaga in a sunny window by tying a string to each nail. As the morning glories grow, they will twine around the string. In many cases the turnip or rutabaga will sprout bright green leaves from its base.

Grass seed is usually plentiful in the spring or fall when people are fixing up their lawns. Sprinkle some grass seed on a sponge and keep it damp so that the grass will sprout. Or collect eggshells to use as tiny planting containers. For this purpose it is helpful to have shells that are broken into uneven halves and to use the larger half. The child fills his eggshell with potting soil, moistens it, and sprinkles the top with grass seed. With felt-tip pens, he can create a face on the shell that will have green hair when the grass seed sprouts.

Perhaps you have sprouted lima or other beans in a glass jar so the children can see what takes place as the plant grows. Besides those, you can make bean sprouts that the children can eat. Mung beans are the easiest to sprout and are available at most health food stores. A half cup of dried beans will make about two cups of sprouts. Soak the beans in water overnight, then drain them and place them in a quart jar. Cover the top with a piece of cheesecloth held on by a rubber band. Put the jar in a dark place and allow the beans to sprout. (Do not try to sprout more than a half-cup of beans in a quart jar because they expand quite a bit. If you want more bean sprouts, use several jars.) To prevent the formation of mold, rinse the beans twice a day by flushing them with water and then pouring the water out through the cheesecloth. The top need not be removed during this process, so it is quickly done. After three or four days, the sprouts are ready to eat. The children may enjoy them as a salad combined with an equal amount of chopped celery and seasoned with a little oil-and-vinegar dressing and soy sauce.

A terrarium is easily made in an old fish tank. Place a layer of sand and gravel in the bottom to ensure proper drainage. Add charcoal to keep the soil sweet. If you will be putting woodland plants in your terrarium, leaf mold should be added next. (Cactus and other succulents would require a sandy soil.) Plant ferns, mosses, and other small plants in the soil. Keep the terrarium in a cool place out of the sunlight. Sprinkle it with water and lay a piece of glass over the top. Do not add more water unless no moisture is forming on the inside of the glass.

Animals in the Classroom

Fish are the easiest animals to keep in the classroom. Even if you are not ready for a more complete menagerie, you need have no hesitation about providing a fish tank for your room. Goldfish are beautiful, inexpensive, and easy to care for, requiring no heaters or other special equipment. Every year in my classroom, the trip to the pet store to buy fish in September was always a big event. (The fish were given away at the end of the year.) To keep goldfish successfully, a bowl is all that is needed, but a tank holds more fish and is more attractive. A ten-gallon tank will support six to eight goldfish. It is a good idea to invest in a pump and a filter, which can be obtained relatively cheaply, because they will keep the water clean and full of oxygen. All you have to do is change the charcoal and glass wool in the filter every two weeks or when it looks dirty. Gravel for the bottom can be purchased for about ten cents a pound, unless you want fancy colors, which are more expensive. You should have at least two inches of gravel covering the floor of the tank.

Be sure to fill the tank with water several days before you purchase your fish. This time allows the chlorine to evaporate. Also, you can purchase at any pet store a liquid to put in the tank to dissipate the effect of the chlorine. The liquid is very useful when you need to add water to the tank after the fish are already in it. This will have to be done about once a month because of evaporation. Plants are not necessary to a fish tank if you have a filter (both supply oxygen) but they add beauty to the tank and give the fish places to hide. The pet store can tell you what varieties are best for goldfish.

The tank should not be placed in direct sunlight. Goldfish like cool water, and the sun might warm the water too much. Also, sunlight will encourage the growth of algae in the tank. A small sponge on a handle, available at most pet stores, is convenient for cleaning the sides of the tank. Also, a net will be needed for removing debris and any fish that do not survive. If you can find a few snails at the pet store, they will be excellent additions to your tank. Because they are scavengers, they will help to keep the tank clean, and their movements up and down the sides of the tank are fascinating to the children.

Fish can be fed any good goldfish food; check with your pet store. Be sure the children do not overfeed the fish. Fish can survive weekends without feeding, but if the holiday is longer than two days, buy special capsules that dissolve slowly and will feed them over several days. Over a longer vacation, the janitors will usually be glad to feed the fish for you, or you can send the tank home with someone.

Another animal that is very easy to care for is a hamster. It is a beautiful little animal and very clean. The only disadvantage is that it is nocturnal, and therefore sleepy most of the time that the children are in school. However, it can usually be roused to eat.

To keep the hamster, you can purchase a wire cage, or you can find a defective aquarium. Pet stores often sell tanks that leak, and so are unsuitable for fish, at quite a discount. Such a tank makes a fine cage if you provide a top. The cage should be at least eighteen inches long by twelve inches wide and twelve inches high—big enough to allow the hamster to arrange his home to his liking. He will make a nest, a food area, and a toilet, and he will use each consistently for the purpose he has assigned to it. For bedding, cedar shavings are clean and fragrant and readily available at pet stores. A water bottle should hang on the side of the cage so that the animal can drink whenever he wishes. The bottle must always be kept full, because a hamster requires a lot of water. It is especially important to be sure that the bottle is filled Friday afternoon, so that he does not go all weekend without water. At pet stores, and in many grocery stores, a mixture of seeds is sold as food for hamsters; also, the children can bring in vegetable parings and pieces of carrots, apples, and even to-matoes, which the hamster will relish as well. An exercise wheel in the cage is a good idea.

Gerbils are similar to hamsters in the ease with which they can be maintained in the classroom, and because they are diurnal animals, there is always a lot of activity for the children to observe. With both gerbils and hamsters, if you keep a pair, you will be deluged with babies at frequent intervals. It does provide the children with a whole course in reproduction, but be sure that you can provide for the babies before you get into the business!

On the basis of one year's experience of keeping a rabbit in the classroom I would say that rabbits are wonderful classroom pets but a lot of work to care for unless you have a very good, easy-to-clean cage arrangement, or unless they can be kept outside. If you are able to arrange the right accommodations (a slide-out cleaning tray, for example, or an outdoor cage) then by all means include a rabbit in your menagerie. Aside from cleaning up after a rabbit, there is little work involved. Water is supplied with a larger version of the water bottle used for the hamster or gerbil. Again, keep water available at all times; rabbits are heavy drinkers. Their basic classroom diet is rabbit pellets, available at feed stores in economical bags. The pellets can be supplemented with occasional carrots, celery, and other vegetables.

Our rabbit was the most popular member of the class and very good natured about allowing himself to be handled. His soft, furry body was very soothing to the children, and they were frequently at his cage petting and talking to him. At first we let him out frequently, but we soon discontinued the practice, primarily because he was not housebroken and the room was carpeted. Also there were thirty-two children in the class, and the rabbit was often in danger of being overwhelmed by their eager hands.

One day when the rabbit was out of his cage, we saw a little boy surreptitiously kicking the rabbit in a corner. It was discovered that he resented the rabbit because it had the same name that he did. Children are naturally curious, active, and frank about expressing their feelings, and they can be overeager in their expressions of affection or resentment towards a small animal. Keeping classroom pets affords an excellent opportunity to help the children learn how to deal with animals and how to express themselves without hurting them. Indiscriminate handling can cause injury and sometimes death to a small animal, and if this happens the child who is responsible will have a heavy burden to bear. It is important that unrestricted playing with a classroom pet as if it were just another toy in the room be discouraged. Instead, children should be taught how to care for the animals and how to handle them properly.

Turtles are interesting additions to the classroom environment. Most turtles you see are kept in shallow bowls of water with a few rocks to climb on. This method allows for easy care, but it is worth the extra trouble to keep your turtles in a small fish tank in about six inches of water where they can dive and swim. This is fascinating for the children to watch.

You will need some sort of floating platform for the turtles to climb out on. Flat styrofoam works well if it is not too thick. Do not bother to beautify the tank with aquatic plants, because the turtles will eat them as fast as you can replace them. A filter and a pump will help to keep the water clean, but you will still have to change the water frequently. You might also buy a small suction tube which enables you to remove bits of debris from the water. Turtles eat packaged turtle food, but to keep them in good health, you should feed them bits of raw meat frequently. The painted turtles sold in stores are babies and will grow quite a bit if they are well taken care of. A light over the tank is beneficial to the turtles' shells, and they like to come out and "sun" themselves under its warmth. The light will encourage the growth of algae, but your long-handled sponge should take care of it if you don't let it get out of hand.

If you want to keep a toad in your terrarium (see page 154) he will need some garden dirt, a water dish, and some stones and grass. A salamander likes moist moss and pieces of decaying wood.

Hatching Chicks

An ambitious project that offers tremendous returns in enthusiasm and learning for the children is hatching hen's eggs in the classroom. It is an exciting process for everyone concerned. An incubator can be built for under twelve dollars. You can obtain directions for the incubator and information about hatching chicks as follows: Outside New York State, write to the Media Services Distribution Center, Cornell University, 7 Research Park, Ithaca, NY 14850. If you are a New York State resident, you can receive copies of the material listed below from your county office of the Cooperative Extension Service Association. There is a nominal cost for each copy. Request the 4-H Poultry Science Incubation Project titled "How to Make a Still-Air Incubator," by E.A. Schano and J.J. Saccente, Leaders' Guide Revised L-8-1a. In addition, ask for Guide L-8-1b, "Incubating Eggs," and C-8-1b, "Incubation/Embryology Chart." Guides L-8-2a, "From the Egg to the Chick," and R-8-2a, "Incubation Data," are supplementary. The local 4-H office was my source for fertile eggs. They were also ready to answer questions whenever I had a problem. The eggs will take twenty-one days to hatch, so try to start your project so they will not hatch over a weekend. (They may hatch at night, but there is nothing you can do about that.)

The incubator should be tested well in advance of the time you are to pick up the eggs. Place a pan of water in the bottom of the incubator. The temperature should stabilize at about 100 degrees Fahrenheit. It should not fall below 97 or go over 103. In fact, these extremes should be avoided. The eggs are particularly susceptible to extreme heat, and even a few minutes at temperatures over 103 will seriously affect the embryo. Once your incubator is adjusted, it should keep a fairly steady heat without your having to do anything further.

Once the incubator has been tested, you are ready to put in the eggs. Before placing them in the incubator, mark each one with an X so you will be able to keep track of which side you turned last. They should be turned three times a day. This duplicates the movement of the mother hen as she shifts her body constantly on the nest and so keeps the eggs from remaining in one position too long. If they remain in one position, the yolk will stick to the shell and the embryo will die. You can get by without turning the eggs over the weekend if you are faithful about it the rest of the time.[1] The children can turn the eggs; it becomes a

---

[1] This is true of hen's eggs. Some other eggs, such as quail, are much more sensitive and do require turning every day.

major event of the day. We held our breath in our room each time an egg was picked up, but the children were extremely careful, and we didn't lose one.

Humidity should be about 50 to 60 percent the first eighteen days, and from 65 to 70 percent the last three. In order to raise the humidity toward the end of the incubation, put a damp sponge in the incubator on the eighteenth day. It should cause some dampness to condense on the view plate. Also, at about this time, place a layer or two of soft material over the wire screen to protect the newly hatched chicks from injuring their tender skin on the wire.

The chicks should be removed from the incubator as soon as they have fluffed up and dried off. Place them in a brooder immediately. A brooder can be easily made from a cardboard box about twenty-eight inches long, twenty-five inches wide, and fourteen inches high. Put two or three inches of litter (shavings, shredded newspaper, or sand) at the bottom of the box. Never place the young birds on a smooth surface such as cardboard, because they won't be able to get a grip, and their legs will splay outward. Place a dish of water in the box. Chickens should be fed chick starter, which is sold at feed stores.

A gooseneck lamp with a 60- or 75-watt bulb provides adequate warmth in the brooder. Bend the lamp closer over the box to provide more heat and move it upward to decrease the heat. (If the side of the box is high, a slit can be cut so that the lamp remains outside the box while the neck fits through the slit.) If chicks are cold, they huddle together. When they are too warm, they spread their wings, open their beaks, and appear to pant. Aim to keep the temperature in the brooder from 95 to 98 degrees. As the chicks grow, you will need to make other arrangements to house them, because they will soon be able to fly out of the brooder. We arranged for a local nature preserve to take the chicks once they were old enough to withstand living out of doors (when their feathers are completely grown.) In the meantime, when they outgrew the brooder, we put them in a spare rabbit cage. Here they had room to move around, yet we were able to keep them warm with the lamp as long as they needed it. Once the feathers have emerged, they no longer need the lamp.

I was amazed at how much the children learned and retained from this experience. We had checked the temperature in the incubator each day to make sure that it was correct, and weeks after the chicks had hatched, the children remembered that the optimum temperature was 100 degrees. We used the experience to talk about all kinds of animals that hatch from eggs. Children sorted pictures of animals according to whether they hatched from eggs or not. Sentences such as "Chickens hatch from eggs." were cut up and the children put them back together again or matched the words to identical sentences that had not been cut up. The children drew pictures of the incubator, the chicks, the brooder, and later the chicks in their cages and told stories about the pictures. Each day, we kept track of how many days had gone by, and how many were left before the eggs would hatch. Sequential pictures of what was happening inside the embryo accompanied the countdown. After the hatch, we made charts noting how many eggs hatched (seven) and how many did not (five), of how many chicks were red, how many were black, etc. A project like this proliferates until it includes every aspect of the curriculum.

Books for Teachers

- Brown, Sam E., BUBBLES, RAINBOWS, AND WORMS: SCIENCE EXPERIENCES FOR PRE-SCHOOL CHILDREN, Mt. Rainier, Md., Gryphon House, 1981.

- Forte, Imogene, and Frank, Marge, CREATIVE SCIENCE EXPERIENCES FOR THE YOUNG CHILD, Nashville, Tenn., Incentive Publications, 1983. PUDDLES AND WINGS AND GRAPEVINE SWINGS: THINGS TO MAKE AND DO WITH NATURE, Nashville, Tenn., Incentive Publications, 1982.

- Rockwell, Robert, *et al*, HUG A TREE AND OTHER THINGS TO DO OUTDOORS WITH YOUNG CHILDREN, Mt. Rainier, Md., Gryphon House, 1983.

■ Sisson, Edith, NATURE WITH CHILDREN OF ALL AGES: ACTIVITIES AND ADVENTURES FOR EXPLORING, LEARNING, AND ENJOYING THE WORLD AROUND US, Englewood Cliffs, N.J., Prentice-Hall, 1982.

Books for Children
PLANTS

■ Bush, Phyllis, LIONS IN THE GRASS, New York, World, 1968.

■ Heller, Ruth, THE REASON FOR A FLOWER, New York, Grosset and Dunlap, 1983.

■ Krauss, Ruth, THE CARROT SEED, New York, Harper & Row, 1945.

■ Leavitt, Jerome and Huntsburger, Jack. FUN-TIME TERRARIUMS AND AQUARIUMS, Chicago, Childrens Press, 1961.

■ Oppenheim, Joanne, HAVE YOU SEEN TREES?, Reading, Mass., Addison-Wesley (Young Scott Books), 1967.

■ Selsam, Millicent E., MORE POTATOES!, New York, Harper & Row, 1972.
PLAY WITH LEAVES AND FLOWERS, New York, Morrow, 1952.
PLAY WITH PLANTS, New York, Morrow, 1949.
PLAY WITH SEEDS, New York, Morrow, 1957.
PLAY WITH TREES, New York, Morrow, 1950.
SEEDS AND MORE SEEDS, New York, Harper & Row, 1959.
While the Selsam books are too advanced to read to kindergarten children, they contain a number of suggestions for activities that can easily be adapted for young children.

■ Shecter, Ben, PARTOUCHE PLANTS A SEED, New York, Harper & Row, 1966.

■ Speer, Bonnie Stahlman, ERRAT'S GARDEN, Chicago, Reilly and Lee, 1969.

■ Udry, Janice M., A TREE IS NICE, New York, Harper & Row, 1956.

■ Whyte, Ron, THE FLOWER THAT FINALLY GREW, New York, Crown, 1970.

■ Zion, Gene, THE PLANT SITTER, New York, Harper & Row, 1959.

ANIMALS

- Darby, Gene, WHAT IS A COW?, Westchester. Ill., Benefic Press, 1957.
WHAT IS A CHICKEN?, Westchester, Ill., Benefic Press, 1957.

- Fisher, Aileen, ANIMAL HOUSES, Glendale, Calif., Bowmar/Noble, 1973.

- Garelick, May, WHAT'S INSIDE THE EGG?, Reading, Mass., Addison-Wesley (Young Scott Books), 1955.

- Hazen, Barbara S., WHAT'S INSIDE?, New York, Lion Books, 1969.

- Heller, Ruth, CHICKENS AREN'T THE ONLY ONES, New York, Grosset and Dunlap, 1981.

- Ipcar, Dahlov, WILD AND TAME ANIMALS, New York, Doubleday, 1963.

- Jackson, Jacqueline, CHICKEN TEN THOUSAND, Boston, Little, Brown, 1968.

- Jaynes, Ruth M., THREE BABY CHICKS, Glendale, Calif., Bowmar (Early Childhood Series), 1968.

- Lauber, Patricia, WHAT'S HATCHING OUT OF THAT EGG? New York, Crown Publishers, 1979.

- Mari, Iela and Mari, Enzo, THE CHICKEN AND THE EGG, New York, Pantheon, 1970.

- McCloskey, Robert, MAKE WAY FOR DUCKLINGS, New York, Viking Press, 1941.

- Schlein, Miriam, KITTENS, CUBS, AND BABIES, New York, W. R. Scott.

- Schloat, G. Warren, Jr., THE WONDERFUL EGG, New York, Scribner, 1952.

- Selsam, Millicent E., ALL KINDS OF BABIES, New York, Scholastic Book Services (Four Winds Press), 1969.
EGG TO CHICK, New York, Harper & Row, 1970.
LET'S GET TURTLES, New York, Harper & Row, 1965.

- Stewart, Bertie, TURTLES, New York, Golden Press, 1962.

- Tensen, Ruth M., COME TO THE PET SHOP, Chicago, Reilly and Lee, 1954.

- Zim, Herbert S., GOLDEN HAMSTERS, New York, Morrow, 1951.

8

art

As children become familiar with different media, they learn to express themselves through drawings, paintings, collages, three-dimensional sculptures, and clay work. These creations may also be the basis for further self-expression through storytelling and creative writing. You can provide many different creative experiences for the children using the materials most commonly found in primary classrooms, along with discarded materials that are easily obtained. You probably have many favorite art projects of your own which can be easily adapted to an informal classroom.

Some projects where the children trace precut patterns or otherwise follow a model to make something, for example, do not encourage creative exploration in the same way that less-structured projects do. But they can be valuable supplements to your art program if they are never a substitute for free experience with many different kinds of materials. In fact, projects that follow a model are particularly good for children whose fine-motor coordination is weak, since the projects do involve tracing patterns and using scissors, hole punches, and staplers. Every time children use their hands for such exacting tasks, the hands are strengthened for later use in writing. Making toy telephones or stuffed gingerbread men is a much more enjoyable way of gaining the necessary flexibility than laboring to hold a pencil and draw circles and lines on a piece of paper.

Parent volunteers can be extremely helpful in running a successful art program, although children can do completely on their own a number of the activities suggested in this chapter, such as crayon-resist or sponge printing once the techniques have been explained and briefly demonstrated at the start of the session. Other activities, such as fingerpainting, go more smoothly if someone is on hand to dish out the paint and to make sure smocks are worn and names put on papers. Still others, like making designs with crayon shavings, or making play dough, definitely require adult supervision because of the equipment that is used. Supervising a popular art project is a particularly good way for a volunteer to break in to the classroom setup, especially if he or she feels a little insecure about beginning.

Tempera

No primary room would be complete without an easel or two, always accessible to the children for painting. But beyond that, tempera can also be used in a variety of printing techniques that give very interesting results and that are fun for children to learn.

Rubber Stamps

Creative Playthings makes a set of rubber stamps that provide a good introduction to printing. The stamps are small plastic cubes with stars, triangles, and various other shapes mounted on them. Children can create interesting designs by repeating and combining shapes. They can be used with stamp pads, but with many children using them the pads soon go dry. A substitute is easily made by placing a piece of sponge in a small aluminum pie plate. Pour a little thinned paint over the sponge and let it sink in. The sponge will provide for quite a bit of stamping before it needs to be refilled. Be sure to have plenty of newspaper on hand so children can blot their stamps before printing.

Natural Materials

A nature walk during the opening days of school will provide a variety of materials for printing. Rocks and leaves will both make interesting prints. For leaf prints, large leaves with distinctive outlines, such as oak or maple leaves, are most successful. The child feels the leaf to determine which is the veined side, since that will produce the most detail in the print. It is painted with a brush and then pressed, paint side down, onto a piece of construction paper. Several prints can usually be made from one painting of a leaf. Rock printing is done the same way.

Vegetable and Fruit Printing

When cut in half, many fruits and vegetables provide interesting textures for printing. Some good ones to use are oranges, lemons, green peppers, cabbages, onions, and potatoes if some sort of design is gouged in the potatoes with a stick before printing.

Sponge Printing

Cut up some old sponges into one-inch or two-inch cubes. Put them on a table covered with newspaper along with small dishes of tempera paint and pieces of manila paper. Children can do sponge printing independently once they are familiar with the technique.

Clay Printing

A small chunk of plasticine is formed into a round ball. To form a printing face, one side of the ball is flattened by pounding it on the table. Interesting textures are added to the face by marking it with sticks, bobby pins, wire screening, or other materials. When the child has made a design he likes, he dips the plasticine in paint and prints. A spongeful of paint is better than a dishful here, because the design will not show up well if the clay is saturated with paint.

For another clay-printing project, each child needs a piece of plasticine and a piece of cardboard four or five inches square. When the clay has been softened by working it in the hands, it is placed on the cardboard and pushed and pressed about until the cardboard is covered with a layer of clay. It should not be completely smooth. Brush the clay lightly with fairly thick tempera. Press construction paper against the clay mat and lift it off. The clay mat can be used over and over again.

Tin Can Printing

This project will need an adult's assistance. A piece of string is wound around a tin can that has been coated with white glue. When it dries, the can is rolled in a dish of paint and then rolled on a piece of paper. A variation is to glue strings of cardboard to the can to form the design.

Cardboard Printing

Arrange scraps of cardboard on a square of cardboard until a pleasing arrangement is achieved. Glue them in place, brush them lightly with tempera, and lay a piece of construction paper on the cardboard. Press down and remove paper.

Wax Paper Printing

Tempera paints can also be used for painting under wax paper, a technique that children find fascinating. You need wax paper, paint, construction paper or manila, and some very smooth paper such as finger-paint paper or oaktag. Give each child a piece of the smooth paper. Drop several blobs of different colors of fairly thick tempera on the paper. Lay a sheet of wax paper over the paint. Now the child manipulates the paint through the wax paper, pushing it around until he is pleased with the design. The wax paper is lifted off and the paper allowed to dry. The process is similar to fingerpainting, but without the messy hands. Some who refuse to fingerpaint because they don't like to get their hands in the paint will enjoy this. The blending of the colors seen through the wax paper has a magical quality. And you can use it to help develop knowledge of how colors blend: red and yellow when pushed into each other make orange. Other prints may be taken off the smooth paper by pressing construction paper onto the painted area and lifting it off. Parchment paper gives a nice effect. Also, you can cut out leaves, flowers, and other shapes from the printed paper and mount them on dark paper.

Crayons

Crayons are another standard feature of every primary room. Most of the time they will be used by the children to make their own drawings, and they should always be readily available along with paper for this purpose. But there are other ways of using crayons which children will enjoy learning.

Crayon Rubbings

Put a shape underneath a sheet of manila paper and rub the side of the crayon (peeled, if necessary) over the sheet. The shape will appear as if by magic. By varying the material placed under the paper, you can provide many different experiences for the children. In the fall, beautiful leaf rubbings can be made by placing leaves under the paper. Stencils can be used: shapes of animals, toys, holiday symbols, and geometric cutouts. Pieces of screening, rubber bands, coins, paper clips, strips of plastic from strawberry boxes, and sandpaper produce interesting effects. As a variation, provide sheets of twelve-inch and eighteen-inch manila paper folded in half and then opened out again. On one half, the child creates a design by pasting scraps of colored paper in an arrangement on the page. Geometric shapes can be used instead of random scraps. When he has finished, the child folds the paper, placing his design on the bottom. Then he rubs a crayon over the blank half facing him. His paper design will appear on the crayoned side. When the paper is opened, he will have two versions of the same design.

Crayon-Resist

A picture is drawn and colored in quite heavily with crayon. Oil crayons are especially good, because they cover more easily than wax crayons. After the picture is well colored, the child covers the picture with a thin wash of tempera. The paint will not adhere to the waxy crayoned areas, but will fill in all other areas, creating a handsome finish. Halloween pictures can be covered with a black wash, deep-sea pictures with a blue wash.

These three projects all require adult supervision:

Crayon Monoprints

Crayon a design on black sandpaper. Place newsprint over the design and iron it briefly. Mount the sandpaper and the print together so the effects can be compared.

Crayon Batik

Make a picture with wax crayons on a piece of cloth such as old sheeting. Be sure that the picture is heavily colored in. Dip the finished pictures into fabric dye, then let dry. When the cloth is dry, press briefly with an iron.

Crayon Shavings

When you have many odds and ends of old crayons, the children can grate them or shave them with a vegetable peeler onto a sheet of waxed paper. Another sheet is placed on top and a warm iron quickly pressed over it. The crayons melt and blend, forming a lovely design. They are particularly effective when hung in a window or some other place where the light can shine through them. They can be placed in frames cut to represent butterflies, flowers, or birds, or as simple free-form shapes.

Collage

You should always have a variety of collage materials available for the children to use as they wish: torn paper, scraps of corrugated cardboard, bits of netting and lace, ribbon scraps, pieces of foil, nylon net, scraps of other fabrics, buttons, and whatever else is at hand. Designs are created by pasting the materials in an arrangement on paper or cardboard. Once the children are acquainted with the technique, they will use it frequently on their own. Two variations of the technique are suggested below.

Mosaics

A group project in the fall begins with a large shape—a leaf, a pumpkin, a ghost—outlined on a piece of brown wrapping paper. The children select poster paper in appropriate colors and tear it into two-inch squares. (Poster paper is thinner than construction paper and tears more easily. It is also much cheaper.) A few children at a time work on filling in the outline. This is a good activity to set up outside the room because it requires no supervision. (When you need to have some paper torn up, try to involve children with poor fine-muscle coordination—it is another excellent way of giving the muscles of their hands some exercise.)

Children can make individual mosaics by tracing or drawing a shape onto a piece of colored paper, and then filling it in with any one of a number of materials. Material for mosaics can be cut or torn from a variety of sources: poster paper, magazine pictures, tissue paper, fabric, wall paper, Christmas cards, and other greeting cards. Three-dimensional pieces can be used also, but when they are the design to be filled in should be sketched on heavy paper, cardboard, or oaktag. Three-dimensional materials might be broken eggshells, pebbles, seeds, straw, buttons, shells, bottle caps, wood-chips, styrofoam scraps, and macaroni and other pastas.

Poster paper in many colors can be made available for tearing and cutting even when no collage work is planned. Children can tear from one sheet of paper to create animal shapes, monsters, and other things. Also, torn paper can be used to complete a design, to put the features on a pumpkin face, or the flowers in a garden.

Fingerpaints

Instead of using shiny fingerpaint paper and putting the paint directly on it, try making a print of fingerpainting. You need a plastic tray or a table surfaced with formica or some other washable material. Dampen the surface of the table and give each child a teaspoon of fingerpaint. After he has moved the paint around on the table and made a design he would like to keep, he takes a piece of manila drawing paper and presses it firmly onto the area he has painted. The paper is removed and allowed to dry. The paint remaining on the table may be sufficient for the next child, or only a little bit more may be needed. You will find that the paper does not curl as it dries the way regular finger-paint paper does. Also, the manila paper gives the design a nice texture.

You might want to try making your own fingerpaint from the following recipe:

    1 cup cornstarch
 2⅔ cups boiling water
    1 cup Ivory flakes or other mild soap flakes
    2 tablespoons glycerine (can be obtained at a
       drug store)
    Vegetable coloring

Make a paste of the cornstarch by adding a little cold water. Add boiling water and cook until thick. While the mixture is still warm, add the soap flakes. Let it cool, then add the glycerine. Add food coloring as desired. It should be about the consistency of stiffly whipped cream. Store in a cool place in covered jars.

Clay and Modeling Doughs

These materials are extremely important for young children to use both because of the manipulation and strengthening of the hands and arms that go on in working with them, and because they provide an extremely fertile ground for self-expression and dramatic play. Often children who show little interest in other art projects will be eager to work with clay.

There is nothing quite like real clay for texture and feel. But it is expensive to use all the time because the children will want to take finished pieces home often, so you will sometimes want cheaper substitutes. The following recipes all provide slightly different materials that can be manipulated and formed into objects. Also, you can keep plasticine in the room and use it over and over again.

Be sure to involve the children in making the clays. Just as in cooking food, important measuring skills are involved, and as much enjoyment can be derived from the preparation of the materials as in using them. You might want to send some of the "recipes" home to the parents so that children could make their own play dough at home.

Hardening Modeling Clay

Combine 2 cups salt with ⅔ cup cold water and bring to a boil. Mix 1 cup cornstarch with ⅔ cup cold water in a bowl and stir until smooth. Add the cornstarch mixture to the salt mixture and cook, stirring, until thickened. Keep in a plastic bag until ready for use. If you wish, you can squeeze food coloring into the cooled play dough and knead it until the color is evenly mixed. Children enjoy helping with this. Or, you can leave it plain and they can paint their objects after they are dry. To have enough dough for thirty children to make an object to take home, you will need to mix up at least three and perhaps four batches. If you are just using it as reusable play dough, one batch may suffice.

Uncooked Modeling Dough

Mix together 2 cups flour, 1 cup salt, and enough water to make a stiff dough. Once blended, the mixture should be thoroughly kneaded. Food coloring can be added or it can be painted after hardening. This dough will harden in about three days.

Bakers' Clay

Mix together in a bowl 4 cups of flour, 1 cup of salt, and 1½ cups of water. If the mixture is stiff, add more water a little at a time. Knead for four to six minutes. Work into desired shapes. Bake on a cookie sheet for one hour or more at 350 degrees. Thick sculptures may take two hours or more. Test for doneness in the thickest part with a toothpick. If it is soft, continue baking. When pieces are cool, paint and decorate. Spray finished pieces with clear fixative to prevent softening. Bakers' clay is particularly good for making flat figures of people or animals for Christmas tree decorations and storybook scenes.

Papier-Mâché

Wallpaper paste is mixed with water to produce a substance with the consistency of heavy cream. Newspaper strips are torn and thoroughly wetted in paste, then smoothed onto a form. The form can be made of balloons or of rolled up newspapers and wire, depending on the shape of the finished object. The form is gradually built up with papier-mâché until the desired shape is attained; then it is left to dry thoroughly before being painted and shellacked. Animals, bowls, people, vases, beads, and puppet heads can all be made in papier-mâché.

Sawdust Mixture

This is a nice pliable material, which is quite light when dry. Add 1 cup of wallpaper paste to one quart of sawdust. Add enough water to make a thick, easily handled mixture. Use immediately.

Snow Suds

Mix 2 cups soap flakes (such as Ivory or Lux; not soap powder) with 1 cup water. Beat with an eggbeater until stiff. The mixture can be spread on cardboard and arranged into mounds of snow. If you make it a little thicker by adding more soap flakes, you can model snowmen out of it.

Crepe-Paper Clay

Cover a table with plastic. Tear one fold of crepe paper into confetti-sized pieces. Put them in a bowl and add enough water to cover. Soak 15 minutes until soft. Drain off any excess water. Mix 1 cup of flour with 1 tablespoon salt and add the mixture to the wet paper to make a stiff dough. Mix it with the hands until well blended. Use soon after mixing.

Junk Sculpture

Have out on a large table an assortment of junk: milk cartons, shoe boxes, wax paper boxes, egg cartons, plastic containers, bottle tops, corks, cardboard tubes, scraps of material, old greeting cards, straws, buttons, rubber bands, string, pipe cleaners, yarn, popsicle sticks, and anything else you have available. Provide the children with white glue, cellophane tape, large brass fasteners, and a stapler. A few suggestions are all that is needed. You will be amazed at the variety of constructions children can come up with. The project is ever popular, and should be frequently available. Sometimes a theme for the construction can be suggested: silly people, rocketships, storybook creatures.

Working with Yarn

To introduce young children to embroidery, use quarter-inch hardware cloth cut into four-inch squares and bind the edges with masking tape. Because the squares would be expensive and time-consuming to prepare regularly, use them only until the children are fairly comfortable with needle and thread. Reuse them by removing the designs at the end of the day. For permanent designs which the children can take home, give them squares of stiffened mesh with six or eight holes to the inch, available from school-supply houses in economical rolls.

For sewing, large yarn needles with blunt tips can be used. The children will probably need help when the needle comes unthreaded, or when they wish to change colors. You may prefer to precut many different colors of yarn ahead of time into ten- or twelve-inch lengths. You can dispense with the need for a needle if you knot one end of each thread and bind the other end with a half-inch square of masking tape to form a stiffened blunt end which will go through large mesh canvas. Or, you can rub white glue on the end of the yarn and let it dry. If you have a parent who would like to help out but cannot come to school because she has young children at home, she might be able to prepare a batch of these yarn cuttings for you if you sent the materials home to her.

The squares of mesh and a variety of yarns are made available for children to use. Some squares might have a simple shape outlined in felt-tip marker as a guide, while others are left blank for the children to fill in as they wish. In addition to mesh squares or hardware cloth, the plastic baskets that cherry tomatoes or strawberries come in can be cut into squares for beginners to use. As the children get more proficient, some of them might enjoy working on burlap or other loosely woven material. An embroidery hoop makes the material easier to work with.

Both this project and the embroidery project just described will go more smoothly if there is an older person available to the children when they run into problems, although some will be capable of working by themselves.

Pleasing yarn designs without needles can be easily made on a simple cardboard frame. You will need to cut out a variety of cardboard shapes—squares, rectangles, triangles—and slit them all around the edge to make a fringe. The cuts should be about half an inch deep and one inch apart. The children take lengths of colorful yarn and wind them around the cardboard frame in any desired pattern, catching the yarn in the slits as they work. Once they have been shown how to do it, they can make the patterns without supervision. If you have an adult available to guide them, small children can make a yarn design known as the Eye of God. Paste sticks, ice cream sticks, or twigs can be used as a frame. The two sticks are bound together in the middle to form a cross.

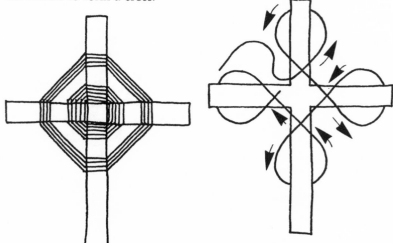

The yarn is wound around each spoke in turn. New colors may be added by holding the end of the old color behind the work and beginning with the new yarn.

Chalk

The children can try drawing on various kinds of textured papers with colored chalk. Gray bogus paper has a rough texture and the colors stand out very well. For wet-chalk painting, the children dip pieces of chalk in water before they draw on paper. The wet chalk is extremely brilliant and gives a jewel-like effect. To prevent the picture from smearing, mix liquid laundry starch into the water used for dipping the chalk. Or the pictures can be sprayed with fixative after they are finished.

Books for Teachers

- Alkema, Chester Jay, COMPLETE GUIDE TO CREATIVE ART FOR YOUNG PEOPLE, New York, Sterling Publishing Co. 1971.

- Bos, Bev, DON'T MOVE THE MUFFIN TINS: A HANDS-OFF GUIDE TO ART FOR THE YOUNG CHILD, Roseville, Calif., Turn the Page Press, 1982.

- Hoover, F. Louis, ART ACTIVITIES FOR THE VERY YOUNG, Worcester, Mass., Davis Publications, 1961.

- Kellogg, Rhoda and O'Dell, Scott, THE PSYCHOLOGY OF CHILDREN'S ART, New York, Random House, 1967.

- Peck, Ruth L. and Aniello, Robert S., ART LESSONS ON A SHOESTRING: NEW IDEAS FOR PRACTICAL ART LESSONS IN THE ELEMENTARY SCHOOL, Englewood Cliffs, N.J., Prentice-Hall, 1968.

- Seidelman, James E. and Mintonye, Grace, SHOPPING CART ART, New York, Macmillan, 1970, 1973 (paper).
CREATING WITH PAPIER-MÂCHÉ, New York, Macmillan, 1971.

- Snow, Aida C., GROWING WITH CHILDREN THROUGH ART, New York, Van Nostrand Reinhold, 1968.

9

songs children like to sing

It has often been said that music is a universal language. Certainly anyone who spends time with young children is aware of the particular appeal that music has for them. There are many times during the school day when singing or music-making can be done: while you are waiting for all the children to arrive in the morning, when the children are feeling restless and unsettled and you want to draw them together, during a bus ride on a field trip, during the cleanup when some children finish ahead of others, or at the end of the day. Even if you feel that you do not have time for a formal music period every day, time that might otherwise be wasted can be put to good use if you and the children spend it singing.

The songs included in this chapter are ones I have found to be especially popular with kindergarten and first grade children—these are the ones they ask for again and again. There are also several songs which can be used in conjunction with the units described in earlier chapters. The bibliography lists several good song books where you may find new favorites to introduce to your children.

If you can read music, you should be able to sing these songs with the children and accompany them with the piano, guitar, or autoharp. A student teacher of mine who felt unsure of herself musically made a tape recording of the piano accompaniments of several songs the children were fond of and then played the recordings as she led the children in song. Children are much more tolerant of your abilities than you are, and they couldn't care less if there are some mistakes as you pick your way through a tune.

These four songs may be learned
as part of a unit on health and the body.

Anatomical Song

Did-n't it rain-a, rain-a, rain-a, rain-a, rain-a, rain-a, rain?

Fine

did-n't it rain, chil-dren? Oh, Lord,_ did-n't it rain?

1. Oh, the toe bone's con-nect-ed to the foot bone; And the

foot bone's con-nect-ed to the an-kle bone, And the

an-kle bone's con-nect-ed to the leg bone; And the

leg bone's con-nect-ed to the knee bone; And the

knee bone's con-nect-ed to the hip bone; And the

hip bone's con-nect-ed to the back bone; Sing-in'

D. C.

"Did-n't it rain, chil-dren? Oh Lord,_ did-n't it rain?"

2. Oh, the finger bone's connected to the wrist
   bone;
   And the wrist bone's connected to the elbow
   bone;

And the elbow bone's connected to the muscle
bone;
And the muscle bone's connected to the shoulder bone;
And the shoulder bone's connected to the neck
bone;
And the neck bone's connected to the head
bone;
Singin' "Didn't it rain, children? Oh, Lord,
didn't it rain?"

Fingers, Nose, and Toes

Words and Tune
Traditional

Put your fin-gers on your nose, then your toes,___

Put your fin-gers on your nose, then your

toes,___ Put your fin-gers on your

nose, Put your fin-gers on your nose, Put your

fin-gers on your nose and then your toes.___

From MUSIC FOR YOUNG AMERICANS (kindergarten). Used by
permission of American Book Co.

2. Put your fingers on your nose, then your cheeks,
   Put your fingers on your nose, then your cheeks,
   Put your fingers on your cheeks and then leave
      them there for weeks,
   Put your fingers on your nose and then your
      cheeks.

3. Put your fingers on your nose, then your hair,
   Put your fingers on your nose, then your hair,
   Put your fingers on your hair and then wave
      them in the air,
   Put your fingers on your nose and then your
      hair.

Head, Shoulders, Knees, and Toes

Head, shoul-ders, knees and toes, knees and toes.

Head, shoul-ders, knees and toes, knees and to - o - es and

Eyes and ears and mouth__ and__ nose

Head, shoul-ders, knees and toes, knees and toes.

Wake Me

Adapted from a
Negro Folk Song

Lively

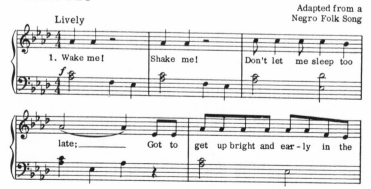

1. Wake me! Shake me! Don't let me sleep too

late;____ Got to get up bright and ear - ly in the

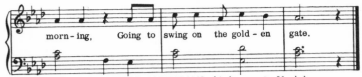

morn - ing,   Going to swing on the gold - en gate.

From MUSIC FOR YOUNG AMERICANS (kindergarten). Used by permission of American Book Co.

2. Wake me! Shake me!
   Don't let me sleep too late;
   Got to comb my hair this morning,
   Going to swing on the golden gate.

3. Got to brush my teeth this morning.

4. Got to dress myself this morning.

Can the children think of other activities?

This is perhaps the most popular song of any that I have ever taught children. A cowboy sings this song to his old horse who cannot accompany him on the long cattle drive.

Good-By, Old Paint

Good - by,   Old   Paint,   I'm   a   leav - ing Chey -
enne.   Good - by,   Old   Paint,   I'm   a   leav - ing Chey -
enne.   My   foot's   in   the   stir - rup; my   pon - y won't
stand.__ Good - by,   Old Paint,   I'm   a   leav - ing Chey - enne.

Good-by, Old Paint. I'm a-leaving Cheyenne.
Good-by, Old Paint. I'm a-leaving Cheyenne.
My wagons are loaded and rolling away.
Good-by, Old Paint. I'm a-leaving Cheyenne.

Good-by, Old Paint. I'm a-leaving Cheyenne.
Good-by, Old Paint. I'm a-leaving Cheyenne.
Good-by, little Annie. I'm bound for Montan'.
Good-by, Old Paint. I'm a-leaving Cheyenne.

This song is popular with children, and they sing it with great gusto. Twice during the years that I taught, a parent came to me upset by the implications of the song, and the fact that the children enjoyed singing it. In both cases, as we discussed it, the parents admitted they had unresolved feelings about the death of someone close to them. Children like this song precisely because it deals openly with death and grief, and yet it is not morbid or gloomy.

Deep Blue Sea

Deep blue sea, ba-by, deep blue sea. Deep blue sea, ba-by, deep blue sea. Deep blue sea, ba-by, deep blue sea.

It was Wil-lie what got drownd-ed in the deep blue sea.

2. Dig his grave with a silver spade.
   Dig his grave with a silver spade.
   Dig his grave with a silver spade.
   It was Willie what got drownded in the deep blue sea.

3. Wrap him up in a silken shroud, etc.
4. Lower him down with a golden chain, etc.
5. Golden sun bring him back to me, etc.
6. Deep blue sea, baby, deep blue sea, etc.

Aiken Drum

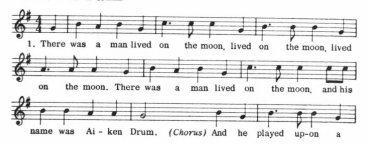

1. There was a man lived on the moon, lived on the moon, lived on the moon. There was a man lived on the moon, and his name was Ai-ken Drum. *(Chorus)* And he played up-on a

la - dle, a la - dle, a la - dle, he played up-on a

la - dle and his name was Ai - ken Drum.

2. His head was made of a pumpkin, a pumpkin, a pumpkin, His head was made of a pumpkin and his name was Aiken Drum. (chorus.)

3. His eyes were made of . . . etc.

4. His nose was made of . . . etc.

5. His arms were made of . . . etc.

This song can continue until you are tired, adding different parts of the body and letting the children suggest what the parts might be made of. The original song uses food, but once that category has been exhausted, you can sing the song using pieces of furniture, animals, or words that start with a particular letter.

The special fascination of this song is the variety of languages in the subsequent verses. Children pick these verses up very quickly, and you may be able to add more if you can find a parent who can translate the verse into a language not included here.

Everybody Loves Saturday Night

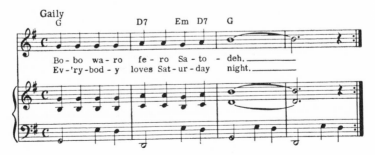

Bo - bo wa - ro fe - ro Sa - to - deh.
Ev - 'ry-bod - y loves Sat - ur - day night.

Bo - bo wa - ro, bo - bo wa - ro, Bo - bo wa - ro, bo - bo wa - ro,
Ev - 'ry-bod-y, ev - 'ry-bod-y, Ev - 'ry-bod-y, ev - 'ry-bod-y,

Bo - bo wa - ro, Fe - ro Sa - to - deh.
Ev 'ry-bod - y loves Sat - ur -day night.

From SONGS OF WORK AND FREEDOM, ed. by Edith Fowke and Joe
Glazer. Used by permission.

1. Bobo waro fero Satodeh,
   Bobo waro, bobo waro,
   Bobo waro, bobo waro,
   Bobo waro fero Satodeh.

2. Everybody loves Saturday night,
   Everybody, everybody,
   Everybody, everybody,
   Everybody loves Saturday night.

3. Tout le monde aime Samedi soir,
   Tout le monde, tout le monde,
   Tout le monde, tout le monde,
   Tout le monde aime Samedi soir.
   (French)

4. Jeder eyne hot lieb Shabas ba nacht,
   Jeder eyne hot, jeder eyne hot,
   Jeder eyne hot, jeder eyne hot,
   Jeder eyne hot lieb Shabas ba nacht.
   (Yiddish)

5. Ren ren si huan li pai lu.
   Ren ren si huan, ren ren si huan,
   Ren ren si huan, ren ren si huan,
   Ren ren si huan li pai lu.
   (Chinese)

6. Vsiem nravitsa sabbota vietcheram,
   Vsiem nravitsa, vsiem nravitsa,
   Vsiem nravitsa, vsiem nravitsa,
   Vsiem nravitsa sabbota vietcheram.
       (Russian)

The donkey in this song is the donkey-engine found on the lumber boats. After they have learned the song, children may enjoy clapping to the chorus. Each child sits facing a partner and they clap the following pattern: clap hands on knees, clap hands together, clap both hands to partner's hands, clap hands together, clap hands to knees. Repeat to the end of the chorus.

Donkey Riding

Canadian Sea Song

Were you ev - er in Que - bec, Stow - ing tim - ber on the deck? Where there's a king with a gold - en crown, Rid - ing on a don - key.

Were you ev - er off the Horn, Where it's al - ways fine and warm? Seen the Lion and the Un - i - corn, Rid - ing on a don - key.

Chorus Joyfully

Hey, Ho! A - way we go! Don-key rid - ing, Don-key rid - ing,
Hey,__ Ho! A - way we go, Rid - ing on a don - key.

From THE OXFORD SONG BOOK, Vol. 2 (Thomas Wood) by permission of the Oxford University Press.

Were you ever in Cardiff Bay,
Where the folks all shout "Hooray"?
Here comes John with his three months' pay,
Riding on a donkey.

This song, and the ones that follow, are other songs which have proved popular with children over the years.

So Long, It's Been Good to Know You

Words and Music by
Woody Guthrie

I've sung this song but I'll sing it a-gain Of the place that I lived on the wild win-dy plain, In the month called A-pril the coun-ty called Gray, Here's what all of the peo-ple there say:—

Chorus

So long, it's been good to know you, So long, it's been good to know you, So long, it's been good to know you, This dust-y old dust is a-get-ting my home,___ And I've got to be drift-ing a-long.___

From SONGS OF WORK AND FREEDOM, ed. by Edith Fowke and Joe Glazer. Used by permission.

Take This Hammer

From SONGS OF WORK AND FREEDOM, ed. by Edith Fowke and Joe Glazer. Used by permission.

1. Take this hammer, (huh!) carry it to the captain, (huh!)

    Take this hammer, (huh!) carry it to the captain, (huh!)

    Take this hammer, (huh!) carry it to the captain, (huh!)

    Tell him I'm gone, (huh!) tell him I'm gone. (huh!)

2. If he asks you, (huh!) was I running, (huh!)
    If he asks you, (huh!) was I running, (huh!)
    If he asks you, (huh!) was I running, (huh!)
    Tell him I was flying, (huh!) tell him I was flying. (huh!)

3. If he asks you, (huh!) was I laughing, (huh!)
    If he asks you, (huh!) was I laughing, (huh!)
    If he asks you, (huh!) was I laughing, (huh!)
    Tell him I was crying, (huh!) tell him I was crying. (huh!)

4. Take this hammer, (huh!) and carry it to the captain, (huh!)

    Take this hammer, (huh!) and carry it to the captain, (huh!)

    Take this hammer, (huh!) and carry it to the captain, (huh!)

    Tell him I'm gone, (huh!) tell him I'm gone. (huh!)

Sweet Potatoes

Soon as we all cook sweet po - ta - toes,
sweet po -ta - toes, sweet po-ta - toes. Soon as we all
cook sweet po-ta - toes, Eat 'em right straight up!

From TWICE 55 COMMUNITY SONGS: The New Brown Book.
Copyright © 1929 by Summy-Birchard Company. Copyright renewed
1957. All Rights Reserved. Used by permission.

Soon as supper's et, mommy hollers,
Mommy hollers, mommy hollers,
Soon as supper's et, mommy hollers,
Get along to bed.

Soon we touch our heads to the pillow . . .
Go to sleep right smart.

Soon's the rooster crow in the mornin' . . .
Gotta wash our face.

Soon's the school bus stops on the highway
Got to go to school.

Soon's the last bell rings in the afternoon,
Got to go right home.

(Or make up a better way to get back where you
started.)

This Old Hammer

1. This old ham - mer_ *(clap in rhythm)* killed John Hen-ry,_
This old ham - mer_ killed John Hen-ry,_

This old ham - mer—

killed John Hen-ry,—   But it won't kill me,

But it won't kill me.

2. This old hammer rings like silver,
   This old hammer rings like silver,
   This old hammer rings like silver,
   But it shines like gold,
   But it shines like gold.

Good Sources
For Songs

■ FIRESIDE BOOK OF AMERICAN FOLKSONGS, selected and edited by Margaret Bradford Boni, New York, Simon and Schuster, 1947.

■ Glazer, Tom, DO YOUR EARS HANG LOW AND FIFTY MORE MUSICAL FINGERPLAYS, New York, Doubleday, 1981.
EYE WINKER, TOM TINKER, CHIN CHOPPER: 50 MUSICAL FINGERPLAYS, New York, Doubleday, 1980.

■ Haines, B. Joan, and Gerber, Linda, LEADING YOUNG CHILDREN TO MUSIC: A RESOURCE BOOK FOR TEACHERS, New York, Merrill, 1980.

■ Landeck, Beatrice, SONGS TO GROW ON, New York, Edward B. Marks Music Corp., 1950.
MORE SONGS TO GROW ON, New York, Morrow, 1954.

■ Seeger, Ruth Crawford, AMERICAN FOLK SONGS FOR CHILDREN, New York, Doubleday, 1948.

■ Winn, Marie, ed., WHAT SHALL WE DO AND ALLEE GALLOO: PLAYSONGS AND SINGING GAMES FOR YOUNG CHILDREN, New York, Harper & Row, 1970.

10

things to make for your room

Following is a series of directions for making some of the things you might want in your room. Many of them are available commercially, but if funds are limited you may want to know how to make them for yourself.

Hundred Board

Materials needed: three-eighths-inch-thick plywood or other wood, twenty-two inches square; 100 five-eighth-inch finishing nails; 100 round key tags.

Sand the edges of the board if it is rough. Rule it off into two-inch squares. Place nails at the intersections, to make ten rows with ten nails in each row. Number the tags from 1 to 100. If you wish, the numerals 10, 20, 30, etc. can be a different color than the others, to emphasize counting by tens.

The child hangs the number tags in order on the board. He can also be given directions for other tasks:

Remove every other tag starting with one (best done with only twenty numbers on the board);

Put up numbers from 10 to 20;

Remove all numbers with zeros;

(With all tags on board) remove the number after 7, before 3, after 21, and so on.

Geoboards

Materials needed: for each board, a piece of three-eighths-inch plywood cut ten inches square; five-eighth-inch finishing nails.

After cutting the board, paint or shellac as desired and let dry. Line it off into two-inch squares using permanent magic marker. A nail is placed at the center of each square. The nail should protrude about three-eighths of an inch. A board ten inches square will need twenty-five nails. If you are making several boards, cut a piece of cardboard ten inches square, rule it off into two-inch squares and punch a hole at the center of each square. This can be used as a template to mark the position for the nails on the boards.

You can also make circular geoboards. Nail twenty-four pins around a circle drawn on a board one foot square. Suggestions for using geoboards are given in chapter 3, page 75.

Balance Scale

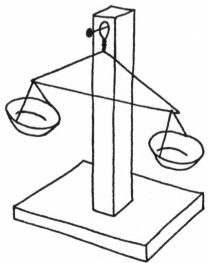

Materials needed: two plastic margarine tubs or small aluminum pie plates; a piece of wood approximately twelve inches by one inch by one-half inch; a piece of wood about three inches square for the base; one wire coat hanger; two nails.

Nail the long piece of wood to the square piece of wood to form a stand. Bend the hook of the coat hanger around to form a small loop. Nail the loop to the top of the stick. It should be fastened loosely enough for the hanger to move freely. Punch two holes in opposite sides of each margarine tub just below the rim. Pass the string through one hole and knot the end. Pass the string over the end of the coat hanger and through the other hole and knot that end. Fasten the second tub in the same way at the other end of the coat hanger.

Number Toss

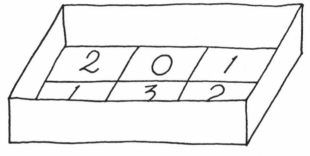

Materials needed: a cigar box or gift box and buttons, bottlecaps, or other suitable markers for tossing.

With a magic marker, draw six squares on the floor of the box as shown. Print a large numeral in each square, keeping the numbers low so that the children can add the results easily. The game is best played with two, but it can be played with more. If you make the game for two, you will need six markers, three each of two different colors.

To play, each child tosses three markers into the box from an agreed upon distance. His score is the total of the numbers he lands on. Each child takes a turn; then the scores are compared. Using toothpicks to keep track of the score will help children who cannot add easily.

Fruit Toss

A matching game can be easily made using a small tin can and small cards with pictures of various objects. A fruit game would use pictures of pears, apples, bananas, and so forth; an animal game would use pictures of tigers, elephants, bears, etc. The cards should have one picture pasted on each side. Six cards can be made for each can. If you make a fruit game, the set of cards might be apple/banana, peach/apple, banana/peach, cherry/pear, orange/cherry, pear/orange. The can itself can be decorated with pictures of fruits, so that, if there are several different games, the children will know where to store the cards for each game.

To play, the child puts the cards in the can, shakes the can, and turns the cards out on the floor. He gets a point for every match that is showing (two pears, two bananas, etc.). Then the cards are placed back in the can and the next child tries.

Ring Toss

Materials needed: a block of wood about three inches square and half an inch thick; a piece of doweling one inch thick and six inches long; scraps of fabric about six inches square; dried beans.

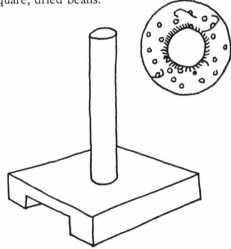

Nail the doweling to the block of wood. Sand the edges and paint. (The children can do this.) To make rings for tossing, cut six circles, six inches in diameter from the fabric. Fold each circle in half. Cut out a smaller circle with a diameter of one and a half inches from each center. You now have six doughnuts. Take two doughnuts, place the right sides of the fabric together, and stitch around the outer edge of the doughnut. Turn to the right side and press. Using a machine zig-zag or close-hand overcasting, stitch around the inner circle, leaving a small opening to put the beans in. Fill the ring with beans, and then stitch the opening closed. Prepare the other two rings the same way.

To play, the child stands a specified distance from the dowel. He scores a point for each of the rings that lands around the dowel. This game and others like it provide good practice in eye-hand coordination and in grasping and throwing.

Concentration

Remember the old childhood card game? The deck of cards was spread out face down on the table, and you took turns turning up two cards at a time. If they matched in number, you could keep them; if not, they

went back into place and the next person drew two cards. The game can be adapted for primary children, for whom it provides excellent practice in matching and visual memory. Depending on the ability of the children, you can use more or fewer cards. For a very simple game, start with eight cards. (Oaktag or shirt cardboard can be used.) The faces of the cards can contain whatever you want: pairs of geometrical shapes, letters, numbers, words, pictures, etc. Just be sure you have a pair of everything you put into the pack.

To play, two or three children lay the cards out face down on the table. The first child picks up two cards, and if they match, he keeps them and draws again. If not, he places them back in the position they were originally, and the second child plays. The game continues until all cards are drawn and matched.

Lotto Games

Many lotto games can be made to develop a variety of concepts. A lotto game is basically a matching game. Several game boards are made up, then smaller cards are made to go with them. One or more children can play. They each take a game board and draw from the smaller cards until one player has matched everything on his board. He is the winner.

Shirt cardboard, oaktag, or other firm surfaces are good for the game boards. A piece of cardboard nine by nine inches can be divided into six squares, each three by four and one half inches. Of course, a larger board can be made and the game will take longer to play. If you coat your boards and cards with the clear plastic adhesive paper now readily available, you will increase their life. You should have several different boards, each with a slightly different arrangement, for each game.

The pictures which go on the game boards and the cards will vary depending on the concept to be developed. A simple game for beginning kindergarten might be a shape lotto. At its simplest, it will have no variant other than shape. (Size and color will be the same, for example.) Each of the six squares on the game board will have a drawing or a cut out shape pasted in it. The game cards will have similar shapes, one to each card. The child has only to match the shape he picks up to the ones on his card, since they are all the same size and color.

A more difficult version uses variation in size and color as well as in shape. The game board might have a small yellow triangle, a large red square, and so forth. In order to get a match, all three qualities would have to be the same.

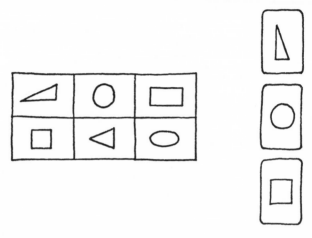

If you have an old wallpaper book, a pattern-matching lotto can be devised. Find similar patterns; often there will be three or four versions of a pattern, each in a different color. The child has to match pattern cards to the patterns on his board. Several patterns should be represented on the various boards, each in several colors. Thus the child has to check two qualities: color and pattern.

Many variations are possible. Pictures of objects whose names start with a particular letter, for example, are a basis for another lotto. The pictures may be cut out of old workbooks or magazines. Reading readiness workbooks usually have a good selection of small pictures representing objects whose names begin with certain sounds. Besides teaching recognition of consonants, this kind of lotto can teach categorizing. All pictures on one board can belong to one category: food, transportation, or toys. The names can be printed below the pictures. For children who can recognize words, a lotto game can be made in which the game boards have objects with their names printed underneath, while the cards contain just the words.

All these variations of lotto provide excellent training in visual discrimination, since the child has to look carefully at the picture to determine if he has a match. If you make up your own games, you can make the task of matching as difficult as you wish. If you have a variety of these games available, children of differing abilities can learn to play them independently.

Often, too, lotto games can be coordinated with a unit. When we were studying birds, I bought two copies of a fifty-nine-cent dime store book with gummed pictures of many different birds with their names printed underneath. With these sets of pictures, I was able to make a lotto that required careful observation of the birds' coloring and features in order to make the match. The children enjoyed this challenging game. In the spring, as we studied about plants and seeds, I made a lotto from two copies of a flower catalog. Here was another game the children enjoyed playing—and some of the matching was quite difficult. Two gladiolas differing just in shades of coloring, for example, offered a real challenge.

Bookbinding

To bind a book so that it more closely resembles a real book involves a lot of work, but it is definitely worth doing now and then because the children are so proud of the results. The method described below was adapted from one presented in a reading course taught by Dr. Charles Reasoner.[1]

1. Take the pages you wish to bind. Cut down a piece of oaktag (an old file folder will do) to the same size as the opened book. (If you want to bind a book that is thicker than eight pages, the oaktag needs to be cut slightly larger than the pages at the sides.)

2. Cut a piece of construction paper the same size as the oaktag. Fold it and place it between the oaktag and the pages of the book. (It will form the end pages in the completed book.)

[1]Dr. Reasoner, a professor in early childhood education at New York University and the author of books on children's literature, gave a course for teachers in Ardsley, New York, primary and elementary schools, titled "Individualized Reading."

3. Open the book to the middle pages. With a needle or thumbtack, punch three holes in the crease: one in the center, and the other two about one and a half inches from the top and bottom edge.

4. Thread a large needle with heavy thread and knot the thread. Working from the oaktag side, push the needle through the middle hole first. Pull the thread to the inside.

5. From the inside, push the needle through the bottom hole. Needle and thread are now back on the oaktag side.

6. From the back, put needle through center hole again, pull through, then push through top hole and pull out.

7. Pull thread tightly and tie securely at center hole.

8. Cut two pieces of shirt cardboard for the front and back of the book. To get the correct size, close the book and place it on the cardboard. Trace around the book.

9. Now prepare the book cover. The best material I have found is plastic adhesive paper. It comes in many patterns and colors and is easier to apply than cloth. A piece twelve by eighteen inches will make a book cover, so you can get three out of one yard. The directions are the same for cloth, except that you would apply rubber cement or glue to the cardboard before smoothing the fabric on.

10. Peel off the protective backing from the adhesive paper. Carefully place the first cardboard sheet down slightly to the right of the middle of the paper. Place the second piece of cardboard slightly to the left of the middle. If the cardboard pieces touch each other, you will not be able to fold them over.

11. Cut away corners as shown.

12. Fold over edges, pressing down well.

13. Now lay sewn book into cardboard covers. First glue the oaktag to the cardboard sections, one on each side. When the oaktag is secure, glue the construction paper to it for the endpapers.

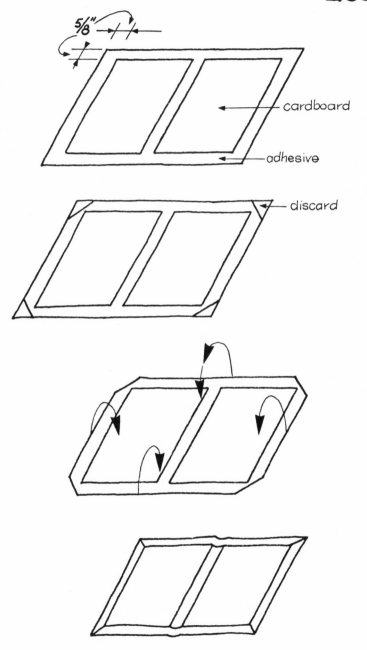

5/8"

cardboard

adhesive

discard

Clown Face for Beanbag Toss

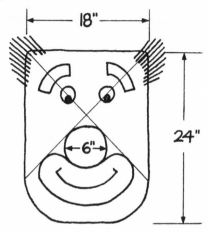

Materials needed: piece of heavy cardboard or masonite one and a half feet by two feet; mat knife (for cardboard) or jig saw (for masonite); tempera paint; yarn scraps.

Following the sketch given above, draw a clown face on the cardboard or masonite. Cut out around the edge of the face, and cut a six-inch circle for the nose. Paint the face, and glue yarn scraps to make hair.

To use the clown face, set it up against a wall or table leg. The children take turns tossing beanbags at the hole.

Inexpensive Slide Viewer

Collect discarded slides from your friends who take photographs. Children particularly enjoy scenes of sporting events, people, animals and birds, boats, cars and trains. Keep the slides organized in boxes labeled with a key word, color, or symbol that also appears on all the slides which belong in that box.

Materials needed:

small frozen orange juice can
dime store magnifying glass to fit orange juice can
two pieces of tri-wall cardboard 3½ inches by 4½
inches (glue two pieces of regular cardboard together if thicker cardboard is not available)
black "mystic tape"
exacto knife
piece of thick inflexible plastic 3½ inches by 4½
inches
masking tape

Paint the inside of the juice can with a dark, nonre-
flecting paint. Trace around orange juice can in center
of each piece of cardboard and cut out holes. Be sure
the holes line up with each other.

Cut a small hole near the rim
of the orange juice can to
accommodate the
handle of the
magnifying glass. Insert
the glass and secure
it with tape.

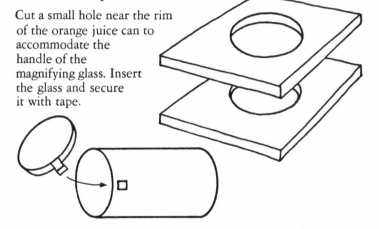

Lay the two pieces of cardboard side by side. Hinge
them with masking tape so that the two pieces can
close like a book.

Open the book. With the knife, cut a two-by-two-inch
square, centered on the hole, on the inside of one
piece, cutting down one-eighth of an inch all the way
around. The slide will fit here.

On the other side of the piece, in which you cut the
space for the slide, tape the piece of clear plastic over
the hole. Force the orange juice can into the hole on
the outside of the other piece of cardboard.

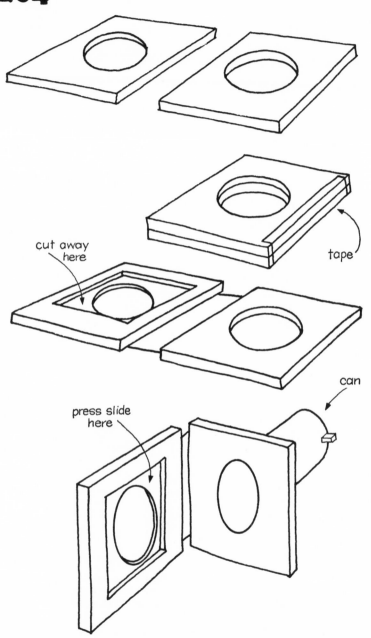

cut away
here

tape

can

press slide
here

cover
plate

tape

To use the viewer, open the
"book," press a slide into
place, close the book,
hold it up to a light
and look at
the slide.

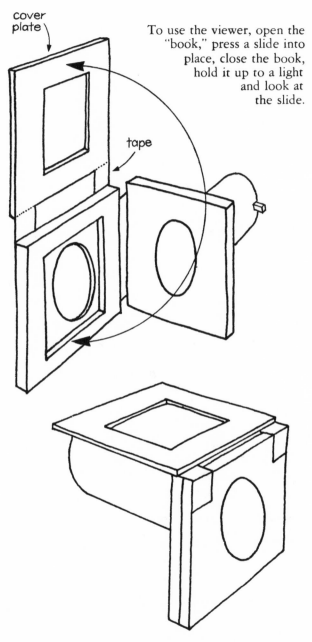

Refinement: to adapt the viewer for filmstrips, make a cover plate of shirt cardboard three and a half inches by four and a half inches. Cut a view hole in the center one and a half inches by one inch. Cover the rest of the cover plate with black mystic tape. Hinge it to the box with two strips of tape, one at each edge, leaving room for the filmstrip to pass between. This can be flipped down over the slide hole. When a filmstrip is to be viewed, flip the cover plate down over the slide hole and slide the strip through the gap between the two hinges. It can be flipped over the top of the viewer when not in use.

Constructing an Electric Board

Materials needed:

2-by-4-foot pegboard
2 "d" flashlight batteries
miniature light bulb and socket
10 feet of insulated bell wire
2 machine screws 1/16 by ¾ inch with nuts
12 round-head machine screws and nuts ½ by 3/16 inch
2 round-head machine screws 2 by ¼ inch
1-by-2-inch wood strips—about 16 feet in all
2 one-inch angle irons
2 #8 ¾-inch flat head wood screws
2 #8 ¾-inch round wood screws
1 spring about one inch long
plasterboard nails
pegboard hangers (to hold cards in place)
several inches of insulating tape

This electric board has space to hang twelve pictures or cards (six pairs) on the front. The spaces are wired to flashlight batteries and to a small light socket. When a child touches a metal probe to the screw next to each of two pictures that belong together, the light goes on, showing him that he has made the correct choice.

To make the electric board, begin by reinforcing the borders of the pegboard with wood strips nailed on with plasterboard nails. (While not strictly necessary, this step will greatly increase the life of the board, which will be in almost constant use.) In the upper left-hand corner of the back of the board, use small pieces of strips to form a box with an inside dimension of five and a half inches. This is to provide space for two flashlight batteries placed end to end, and will also allow for a spring to be inserted to hold them in place. Next, in each end of the box fasten an angle iron. They are to provide the metal contact needed to transmit current from the batteries to the light. The angle irons are fastened to the box frame with wood screws. To the angle iron at the outside edge of the frame (A) attach a three-foot length of bell wire. This is done by bending the bared end of the wire around a roundhead wood screw, on which a steel washer has been placed. Then the screw is tightened up. To the angle iron on the inside edge of the box, attach a twelve-inch piece of bell wire, again bending the wire around a round-head screw, and tighten the screw.

Take the three-foot and the twelve-inch lengths of bell wire that have been fastened to the angle irons and run them through holes in the pegboard to bring them out on the front side of the panel. Next, attach the minia-ture light socket to the front top center of the panel, using three-fourths- by one-sixteenth-inch machine screws. After the light socket is installed, fasten to its left hand connection the twelve-inch length of bell wire that comes from the angle iron on the back of the panel. Complete the wiring of the light socket by fastening a three-foot length of bell wire to the right-hand connection. When this is done, you will have two dangling three-foot lengths of bell wire. One is at-tached to one of the angle irons in the battery box, and the other is fastened to one of the connections on the miniature socket. Scrape the insulation off the loose end of each of these wires and wind each of them around the head of a two-inch machine screw. Hold the wire in place by tightening up the nut as far as it will go. Wrap all the machine screw except the lower half inch with plastic insulation tape.

The two long wires with the machine screws at their ends are now the probes, which the child is to use to make the light go on. The light will go on when the proper pair of screw heads are touched to complete the electrical circuit.

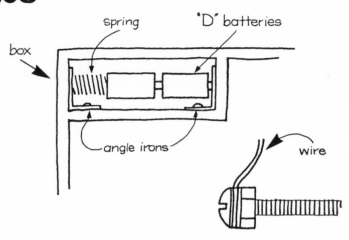

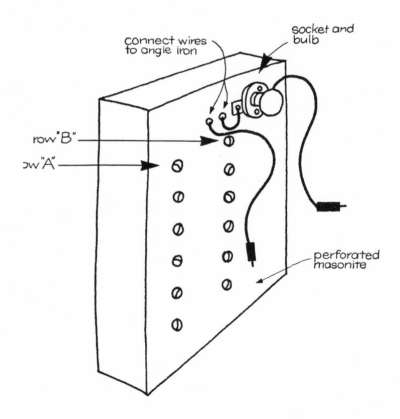

box

The next step is to install the connections on the peg board. This is done by inserting six half-inch-long machine screws evenly spaced down the left side of the board (row A in the diagram), and then placing six more in a row down the middle (row B). Turn to the back of the board. Cut your remaining bell wire into six pieces, each about fifteen inches long. After scraping the insulation off both ends of each wire, attach each piece to the back of a machine screw in row A and to one in row B. This is done by first placing a steel washer on the machine screw. Then bend the bell wire around the screw, put on the nut, and tighten it.

The wiring pattern will need to be changed from time to time, since the children will begin to memorize which connections always "work." When this happens, simply rewire the back in a different pattern.

Fit the batteries into the box on the back of the panel and insert the spring to hold them in place, thus insuring that contact is made. Now your board is almost ready to use. Screw a light bulb into the socket and test the connections. If the light does not go on, tightening all the screws around the wires should help.

If you want to hang your board instead of leaning it against the wall, insert two screw eyes in the top and put heavy twine through them.

Next to each of the screw heads on the front, insert two pegboard hangers two or three inches apart. Your pictures will be hung here. These cards are cut from cardboard or oaktag and have two holes punched at the top so they can be suspended on the board.

Suggestions for cards:

capital letters .... small letters
squares of colored paper . color words
numerals .... numbers of objects, cutouts, etc.
vocabulary word .... picture (tepee ⩎)
animal mothers .... animal babies
initial consonants .... pictures of things beginning with different sounds
pairs of rhyming pictures

Bibliography

■ Breyfogle, Ethel, *et al*, CREATING A LEARNING ENVIRONMENT: A LEARNING CENTER HANDBOOK, Santa Monica, Calif., Goodyear Publishing, 1976.

■ Collier, Forte, *et al*, KIDS' STUFF KINDERGARTEN AND NURSERY SCHOOL, rev. ed., Nashville, Tenn., Incentive Publications, 1982.

■ Farrow, Elvira, and Hill, Carol, MONTESSORI ON A LIMITED BUDGET: A MANUAL FOR THE AMATEUR CRAFTSMAN, Los Angeles, Educational Systems Publications, 1975.

■ Kaplan, Sandra, *et al*, A YOUNG CHILD EXPERIENCES: ACTIVITIES FOR TEACHING AND LEARNING, Santa Monica, Calif., Goodyear Publications, 1975.

■ Lorton, Mary Baratta, WORKJOBS: ACTIVITY-CENTERED LEARNING FOR EARLY CHILDHOOD, Menlo Park, Calif., Addison-Wesley (School Division), 1972. This book contains ideas for many independent activities for nonreaders and beginning readers. The activities can be made easily and inexpensively.

■ Nelson, Leslie W., INSTRUCTIONAL AIDS: HOW TO MAKE AND USE THEM, Dubuque, Iowa, Wm. C. Brown, 1970.

appendix

a

the child
with
learning
problems

The question of how to deal with the children in your classroom who have learning disabilities cannot be adequately treated in a book of this kind. Enlightened school districts are hiring specially trained people to help classroom teachers work with children with learning difficulties. Also, prekindergarten screening sessions can help to identify children who may have problems, so that the teacher can be alerted to their needs right at the beginning of the year. Several books are listed below which may aid you in helping the child with special problems in eye-hand coordination, auditory memory and discrimination, visual memory and discrimination, gross motor skills, and other areas. You must be careful to give the child with special problems help in these areas without exposing him to the frustration and despair he can feel when he sees other children doing easily what he cannot do. Poor self-image, short attention-span, and behavior problems can result when the special needs of learning-disabled children are not met. In a large class, it is difficult for a teacher to attend to each child as she would like, but many activities which are already a part of your program, or are suggested in this book are especially relevant to learning problems. As examples, I have listed activities which are appropriate to children with weaknesses in two areas: gross motor skills and fine motor skills. A good reading-readiness program contains numerous activities in auditory and visual perceptual skills appropriate to children whose special needs are in those areas. In addition, the books suggested for further reading give a thorough treatment of the whole subject and are recommended for anyone who seriously wants to learn more about learning disabilities.

Suggested Activities for Development of Gross Motor Skills

Working with beanbags and balls of various sizes: catching, throwing, rolling, and grasping;

Exercising on a mat: rolling over, crawling, simple tumbling;

Using the balance beam: Walking with eyes open, eyes closed, hands out, hands at side, big steps, and small steps; crawling on beam, walking sideways;

Using the large number-line: following-directions games as suggested in Chapter 3;

Using rhythm instruments, marching to music;

Developing body awareness: learning names of parts of the body;

Playing simple follow-the-leader games involving moving different parts of the body on command (lift your right leg and your left arm, put your hand on your knee, etc.)

Suggested Activities for Development of Fine Motor Skills

Cutting, pasting, working with clay;

Using templates and stencils;   Stringing beads;

Outlining and coloring shapes;

Doing simple dot-to-dot exercises (first at the chalkboard, then on paper);

Doing simple weaving and embroidery;

Lacing and hole-punching. The child can be given a selection of shapes to trace. He traces one on oaktag, cuts it out, and punches holes around the edge. The yarn is then laced in and out of the holes;

Picking up and sorting activities: button box; sorting nails, nuts, and screws; putting pennies into a bank; using marbles; playing pick-up sticks; holding clothespin races (wooden pinch-type clothespins are clipped onto the edge of a cardboard box; the child tries to get as many on as he can in a given time. He can try with both hands to see which can do better);

Folding and tearing paper;   Using pegboards;

Working with design cubes, parquetry blocks, and parquetry designs.

For Further Reading

- Arena, John I., ed., TEACHING EDUCATIONALLY HANDICAPPED CHILDREN, San Rafael, Calif., Academic Therapy Publications, 1967.

- Cruickshank, William, THE BRAIN-INJURED CHILD IN HOME, SCHOOL, AND COMMUNITY, Syracuse, N.Y., Syracuse University Press, 1967.

- Ellingson, Careth, THE SHADOW CHILDREN: A BOOK ABOUT CHILDREN'S LEARNING DISORDERS, Chicago, Topaz Books, 1967 and New York, Harper & Row, 1970.

- Farnham-Diggory, Sylvia, LEARNING DISABILITIES: A PSYCHOLOGICAL PERSPECTIVE, Cambridge, Harvard University Press, 1978.

- Kephart, Newell, C., THE SLOW LEARNER IN THE CLASSROOM, Columbus, Ohio, Charles E. Merrill, 1971 (2nd ed.).

- Lowell, Adgar, and Stoner, Marguerite, PLAY IT BY EAR: AUDITORY TRAINING GAMES, Los Angeles, John Tracy Clinic, 1963.

- Noyes, Joan, YOUR CHILD CAN WIN: STRATEGIES, ACTIVITIES, AND GAMES FOR PARENTS OF CHILDREN WITH LEARNING DISABILITIES, New York, William Morrow, 1983.

  Although written for parents, this book provides a good overview for teachers, as well as an extensive section of games and activities for the LD child which are also suitable for the classroom.

- Painting, Donald H., HELPING CHILDREN WITH SPECIFIC LEARNING DISABILITIES: A PRACTICAL GUIDE FOR PARENTS AND TEACHERS, Englewood Cliffs, N.J., Prentice-Hall, 1983.

- Valett, Robert E., THE REMEDIATION OF LEARNING DISABILITIES: A HANDBOOK OF PSYCHOEDUCATIONAL RESOURCE PROGRAMS, Belmont, Calif., Fearon Publishers, 1967.

appendix
b

prekindergarten testing

There are several benefits of a prekindergarten testing program. The program enables the people who will be most directly concerned with the child as he enters school to see him on an individual basis before he enters school in September. The child has a chance to visit the school, see the kindergarten rooms, and meet the teachers. The one-to-one conference with each parent establishes the foundation of the family's relationship with the school. And the testing provides a means of evaluating the child's developmental level so that his needs can be cared for as early in the year as possible.

The testing program described below was developed by Dr. Brad Doane, Director of Pupil Personnel Services, Ardsley Public Schools, Ardsley, New York, and carried out under the direction of Mrs. Imogene St. Paul, principal, at Ardsley Primary School and subsequently at Westorchard School in Chappaqua, New York.

At a special meeting in the spring, parents are informed of the purposes of the testing and of the procedure to be followed. Appointments are set up for late May and June so that each child who will be entering kindergarten in the fall comes to school with one or both parents for a thirty-to-forty-five-minute period.

When the child and his parents arrive for the interview, they are introduced to the school psychologist and to a kindergarten teacher who has been relieved of her classroom duties for the day by a substitute. Then the child goes with the psychologist for the testing, and the mother and/or father goes with the teacher for an interview. In most cases the child will go off with the psychologist without reluctance. But if he shows any anxiety, the mother remains with him during his session with the tester. In many cases, once the child is involved in the activities, the parent can slip away unnoticed. Children who are extremely fearful and unwilling to leave their mothers at all are often the children who will be nervous and unhappy at the beginning of the school year. When the teacher is aware in advance of who these children are, she is often able to head off problems by devoting extra care and attention to them during the first few days of school in the fall.

The psychologist begins by asking the child his name, address, phone number, birthday, and the names of his brothers and sisters. While all this information is available from the parent, the psychologist's survey reveals much about a child's awareness and level of maturity. The child is given the Peabody Picture Vocabulary test. Without requiring the child to speak, the test measures intelligence as it is reflected in the development of vocabulary. The child is asked to reproduce a set of designs of varying complexity (see the sample at the end of this appendix.) To check his concept of number, the child is asked to count to ten, and to select three, five, seven, nine, and then six from among a group of blocks. He is asked to name the number before nine and after thirteen, and he is given a set of toys and asked to sort them into groups (eating utensils, farm animals, and vehicles, for example). Next, the child is given a set of plastic shapes and asked to sort them. After he has sorted them one way, by color or by shape, he is asked if he can sort them in another way.

A brief test of the child's auditory discrimination is given when he is asked to point to pairs of pictures as called for by the examiner. Finally, the child is asked to draw a picture of a man. The drawing is rated immature, average, or mature (or gradations in between) according to how well it is proportioned, integrated, and detailed.[1]

As the examiner conducts the test, he notes the child's approach to the tasks, his relationship to the examiner, his handedness, gait, and posture. All of these observations help the examiner to make conclusions about the child's social and emotional maturity.

The interview with the parents is conducted with the interview sheet as a guide. (See the sample sheet at the end of the appendix.) Any additional comments made by the mother or father are noted by the teacher. If a friendly, informal atmosphere is maintained, parents will sometimes feel free to express fears, hopes, or observations about the child that will be of great benefit to the teacher, but which would never be recorded on a standard entrance form.

After the interview of the parents and the testing, the child and parent visit the school nurse. She asks the child to perform a few simple tasks, such as walking on a balance beam, catching a ball, and copying a rhythm on a drum. (A sample of the nurse's evaluation sheet is included in the appendix.) In addition, she tests the child's vision and hearing. The parent gives to the nurse a developmental history of the child which has been filled out by the parents and the family doctor.

At the end of the day, the teacher, nurse, psychologist, and principal meet to discuss the results of the day's testing. On the basis of the information that has been collected, notes are made indicating the types of experiences for which each child seems ready, the climate in which they can best take place, and what the teacher's approach to the child might be. Children who will need special help from the speech teacher, the learning-disabilities teacher, or the physical education teacher are identified, so that necessary special help can be scheduled as early in the fall as possible. A

[1]The Metropolitan Readiness Test manual offers guidelines for analyzing the drawings.

folder for each child is assembled, containing the psychologist's interview record, the parent interview record, the nurse's evaluation, the developmental history, the child's drawing of a man and his reproduction of the designs, and the notes produced by the conference about the child. All of this information is made available to the kindergarten teachers as they prepare for their new classes.

Guide to Parent-Teacher Conference[1]

CHILD'S NAME _____

SOCIAL HISTORY

Describe his relationship with other children. _____

How old are most of his playmates? _____
Describe his relationship with his parents. _____

What is his attitude toward strangers? _____

Has he had previous group experience? _____
Nursery School _____ Other _____
What are the major events of his life recently? (moves, travel, etc.) _____

EMOTIONAL STATUS

Describe his temperament. _____
How does he react to discipline? _____
What discipline works best with him? _____
How does he react to new things, and changes in routine? _____
Describe his ability to play by himself. _____
What activities does he choose when alone? _____
What things does he still need to have done for him?

Does he prefer to do things for himself when he is able? _____

[1]The teacher uses these questions as a guide in helping her conduct the interview, which should be as informal as possible.

LEARNING POTENTIAL
Parent's impression

Estimate of child's intelligence. _____
How does child learn things? _____
What is his attention span for a quiet activity? _____
What school activities can child already perform?
    Knows alphabet _____ Writes name _____
    Other _____
What do you consider the child's chief strength as a person? _____
In what areas would you like to see your child stronger? _____
What behavior or aspects of growth have you found most difficult to handle? _____
_____

Do you ever have difficulty understanding your child's speech? _____
Does your child need special care for any reason? ___
_____

Other notations _____
_____
_____
                         TEACHER _____
                         DATE _____

Guide to Psychologist's Interview

Name _____ Date _____
Street _____ Time _____
Phone _____ Birth date _____ Age __
Nursery School _____ Siblings _____

_____

Peabody Picture Vocabulary: AS __ II __ Quintile __
Visual Motor: Figure 1__ 2__ 3__ 4__ 5__ 6__ 7__
Number Concept: Counting (10+) _____
3,7,6,5,9 _____
Number after 13 and before 9 _____
3+1_____ 2−1_____ More (3 vs. 2)_____
Classification A. Instruction _____ Relationship _____
    B. Color _____ Shape _____
Auditory Discrimination _____
Visual Discrimination _____
Draw-a-man: Immature Average Superior
Emotional-social maturity:
  Separation from parent _____
  Relationship to examiner _____
  Approach to task _____
Handedness _____ Holding crayon _____
Coordination _____ Speech _____
Comments: _____
_____
_____

     Examiner _____

Guide to Nurse's Evaluation

CHILD'S NAME _____
DATE _____

A. BALL ACTIVITY
   1. Bouncing:
     Child catch _____ Child bounce to nurse _____
   2. Throwing:
     Child catch _____ Child throw to nurse _____
B. HOPPING
   1. Right foot _____
   2. Left foot _____
C. BALANCING
   1. Walking balance beam _____
   2. With eyes closed _____
   3. On left foot _____
   4. On right foot _____
D. REPEATING RHYTHM ON DRUM
   1. Two short and one long _____
   2. Three short _____
E. IDENTIFICATION OF BODY PARTS
   1 "Touch your ears" _____
   2. "Touch your nose" _____
   3. "Touch your feet" _____
   4. "Touch your shoulders" _____
F. TOOTH DEVELOPMENT _____
G. EYE ACUITY _____
H. EAR ACUITY _____
I. OTHER _____

Designs
for
the Child to
Reproduce

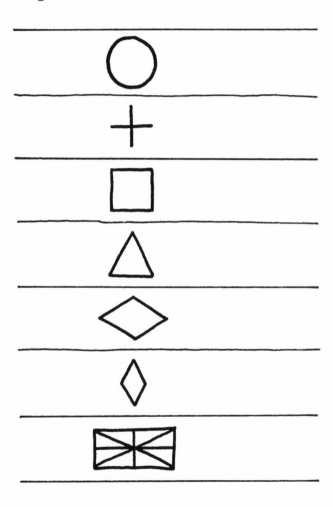

appendix

C

materials
to collect
for your classroom

toilet paper rolls
paper towel rolls
shirt cardboard
corrugated cardboard
gift wrap paper
greeting cards
aluminum foil
empty spools
bottle caps
milk cartons
egg cartons
popsicle and ice cream sticks
toothpicks
small boxes
playing cards
fabric scraps
yarn
ribbons
lace
rickrack
buttons
wallpaper books

carpet samples
corks
wood scraps
sawdust
pieces of styrofoam
excelsior, other packing materials
old picture books
calendars
magazines
seed catalogs
trading stamp catalogs
oatmeal and salt boxes
aluminum pie tins
plastic berry baskets
styrofoam meat trays
wire screening
hardware cloth
coffee cans and lids
plastic bottles
jar tops
spray can tops
plastic margarine tubs and tops
balloons
old clothes and accessories for dress up: hats, ties, veils, shoes, belts, purses

index

3 1543 50141 2888

372.13
R859t

DATE DUE

WITHDRAWN

Cressman Library
Cedar Crest College
Allentown, Pa. 18104

DEMCO